SOLO CANOEING

Other Books by John H. Foshee

Alabama Canoe Ride and Float Trips
You, Too, Can Canoe
Little River Canyon, Grand Canyon of the South

SOLO CANOEING

A Guide to the Fundamentals, Equipment, and Techniques for Running Rivers Solo in an Open Canoe

John H. Foshee

Stackpole Books

Copyright © 1988 by John H. Foshee

Published by
STACKPOLE BOOKS
Cameron and Kelker Streets
P.O. Box 1831
Harrisburg, PA 17105

Printed in the United States of America

10 9 8 7 6 5 4 3 2 1

Library of Congress Cataloging-in-Publication Data

Foshee, John H.
    Solo canoeing: a guide to the fundamentals, equipment, and
techniques for running rivers solo in an open canoe / John H.
Foshee.
        p.   cm.
    ISBN 0-8117-2281-3
    1. Canoes and canoeing.   2. Canoes and canoeing–Equipment and
supplies. I. Title.
GV783.F77   1988
797.1'22'028–dc19
                                                    88-2444
                                                    CIP

To my Mama—
because she is;
to Greig and Carole
and
to Shirley

Contents

Foreword

People take up solo canoeing for various reasons and at different times in their canoeing careers. Some start off solo and are utterly at a loss when confronted with another body in their canoe; others learn to paddle tandem then switch to solo (the method I think is best and the one that seems the most prevalent); still others intermix the two styles according to time and circumstance.

Some paddlers simply seem to have no desire to share their canoe. Possibly past circumstances have consistently left them partnerless and thus conditioned them to the solitude and majesty of paddling alone. Possibly an unfortunate string of partner choices has convinced them that *anything* beats two in a canoe. Others may have a solitary nature or natural disposition that renders them unfit for the social niceties inherent in a tandem setup. Then, of course, there are those who simply prefer the various rewards of solo canoeing and are willing to accept the small payment its disadvantages demand.

Solo canoeing does indeed have its rewards. The solo canoeist is freed from the search for a partner, from the disappointment of a trip missed because a partner couldn't go, and from the idiosyncrasies of another personality. The canoe itself, being more lightly loaded, is easier to paddle, faster, more maneuverable, and has a shallower draft.

On the other hand, these rewards have their price. Some techniques are a little harder to do solo than tandem, loading and unloading the solo canoe and equipment is often strictly a one-person job, and there are times when the extra strength of a bow person would come in handy—sometimes in maneuvers, sometimes in paddling long, flat stretches. And of course, there is no one else to blame for mistakes; the solo canoeist receives what glory there may be, but is also alone with any error!

Ideally, I suppose, all paddlers could have a 50-pound bow person, tremendously strong and long-armed, who could be made to appear and disappear at will. This would solve everybody's problems and satisfy both tandem and solo enthusiasts. However, as this is not within the current realm of possibility, we will all have to be content with our choices. Since you are reading this book, I assume your present choice is solo.

So . . . happy paddling and let's get to work!

Introduction

This is not the world's thickest book, as you may have noticed. That's because this is not a compendium on canoeing in general, but is instead dedicated specifically to the techniques of solo canoeing and even more specifically to solo canoeing in rivers. All the information you need to get started in solo paddling is here, even if you've never *seen* a canoe before, much less paddled one. I've omitted a lot of "why-it-works" explanations and concentrated more on the "how-and-when-to-do-it" type reasoning. If you would like in-depth explanations of "why," I suggest you get a good tandem canoeing book and absorb from it those other various details that you should know, but are not essential to your basic paddling ability or safety.

Obviously, no single book can cover every variation of paddling technique. Although the Red Cross and the American Whitewater Affiliation (AWA) have tried to "standardize" paddling techniques and nomenclatures and I have, in general, gone along with their efforts, you will find some variations from their recommendations of names, styles, and presentations in this book and still others if you journey round the country. In truth there is no one single standard, nor is there likely to be as long as paddlers are cast from different molds.

Similarly, no one book can cover every river situation. These two "lacks" in any canoeing book sometimes present problems to beginning canoeists, who often expect clear-cut black-and-white answers to every question. Already absorbed in conquering the basics, they haven't the time to take in a lot of nuances or the experience to recognize their worth. All that can be done is to give clear-cut methods and let experience and experimentation take care of the nuances.

You will also find, as you go through this book and study its contents, that the results (and successes) of some suggestions and descriptions of techniques will vary depending on the boat you are paddling when you try them. This is because the book is written for both the paddler who wishes to go solo in a full-size, basically flat-bottomed "cruising" canoe as well as the one who ventures out in a 30 pounds lighter, two feet shorter, narrow, rockered slalom canoe – the two hulls just do not react the same, and your techniques will have to be somewhat adapted to the "hotness" of your specific canoe.

That's what I've tried to do in this book: give workable, generally accepted methods that cover the fundamentals of solo paddling and maneuvering. It will take work and study to glean all the information and it will take practice to translate it to practical paddling. Believe me, however, there *are* reasons for everything. Holding a paddle perpendicular to the water during a forward stroke, for example, is not just a personal whim; there's a scientific, physical principle involved that will increase your forward stroke efficiency and reduce the effort you exert for a given effect.

Obviously there are some ifs, ands, and buts. There always are exceptions to rules. I was once asked by a slightly puzzled student if there were ever any "definites" in canoeing. The answer to that is a qualified *yes*, for there are definites under one condition and other definites under other conditions, and they may not be interchangeable. In my tandem book, *You, Too, Can Canoe,* I referred to this situation, the difficulty of explaining it, and the resulting necessity of using "weasel" words. You'll find some of these weasel words in this book too, for many times *you* will have to decide what's definite, when it's definite, and if that definite fits your canoeing requirements.

And that's as definite as I can get!

1

The Solo Canoe

Any canoe can be paddled solo. Whether the paddling gives the most fun and best fulfills the unique pleasures of solo paddling, however, is something else again. Obviously some canoes are better suited for it than others. Exactly what boat you paddle solo is dependent on a number of factors, some more important than others. The foremost factor is, what boat do you now own? For this is where most people start their solo careers – in whatever craft they possess when the mood strikes them to try it. There is nothing wrong with this, unless you happen to own a barge laboring under the delusion it's a canoe, or an equally misguided square-stern canoe. In either of these cases you are likely to become discouraged at an early date. In sum, there are a few guidelines to follow in choosing (or using) a solo boat.

Dimensions and Designs

Double or Single End

There is no doubt a double-ended solo canoe is preferable to one with a square stern. While square-stern canoes *can* be paddled solo,

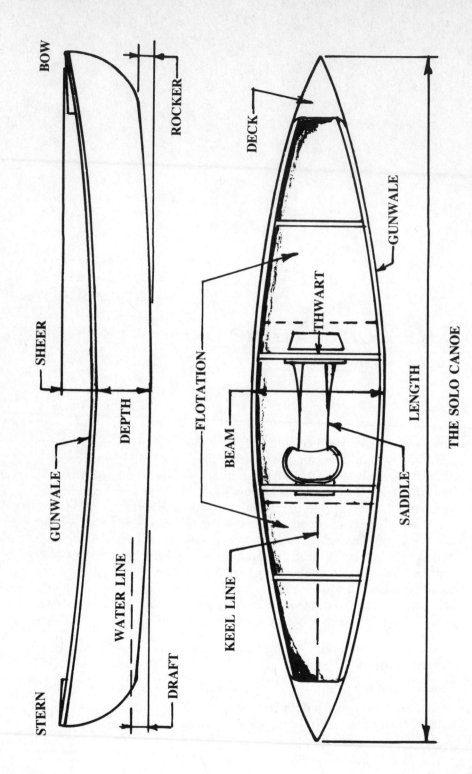

THE SOLO CANOE

they present some very real disadvantages when put to river and whitewater usage – the common stomping grounds of the solo paddler.

Length

Broadly speaking, a hull about 16 feet long is nearing the maximum desirable length for solo river use, at least for us mortals of normal size. Longer boats *can* be handled solo, but unless the paddler is a veritable hulk of muscle, the boats are neither very maneuverable nor very much fun. There is one obvious exception: a solo paddler making a long-distance cruise with a lot of gear. But this usage is not the primary object of this book.

Canoes designed for solo river work (slalom canoes) and whitewater paddling are usually about 13 to 15 feet long. Such lengths provide some balance of maneuverability, responsiveness, stability, and safety. However, this does not preclude using your regular old 15- to 16-foot cruising canoe.

Weight, Width, and Depth

With all else being equal, shorter, lighter, narrower canoes respond better in solo work. In exchange for this response, the solo paddler sacrifices some stability and weight capacity.

Most slalom boats are about 27 to 30 inches wide; cruising canoes average 34 to 36 inches. Pure solo boats also have lighter hulls. This is partially a product of reduced length and width, partially because of their material and manufacturing (at least in the better brands), and partially by design. "Lighter" in this case means about 30 to 60 pounds per hull as compared to the 16-footer's more average 65 to 80 pounds. Any canoe needs enough depth so it doesn't dip its gunwale every time the hull heels over a little. Current depths on solo boats range about 12 to 14 inches. In this respect they're not much different from most cruising canoes.

Hull Shape

Recent years have seen the advent of much more sophisticated canoe hull designs than the traditional old flat-bottomed, rounded-bilge, symmetrical hull with tumblehome. The current emphasis is on two things: rocker and the V bottom.

Rocker is how much the bottom of the boat rises up at the bow and stern above the lowest point of the hull. To some Indians (nothing is really new under our sun) such rockered craft were known as "broken back" canoes, which is sort of what a highly rockered boat looks like. Rocker is where the genuine slalom, solo river canoe begins to pull away from its flat-bottomed cruising relatives. Any canoe tends to pivot on whatever part of it is lowest in the water. With rocker in a hull, starting about the midpoint of the length, this midpoint becomes the basic pivot point of the whole canoe. Add the solo paddler's weight—typically near the longitudinal center of the boat—to this same point and the canoe, in effect, becomes balanced on a pin. The more rocker, the finer the pin. Eventually, as one paddler put it, "you don't have to do anything to turn the boat, you just *think* it!" Maybe a little exaggerated—but not much.

Balancing on a pin, however, in a short, narrow, light boat requires some finesse, practice, and a good sense of equilibrium. Rocker reduces the amount of hull in the water and thus the boat's stability, so there is a point beyond which you may not wish to tread. The amount of rocker varies from manufacturer to manufacturer but, in general, the "hotter" the slalom boat, the greater its rocker.

The other design trend is the V bottom. While this may appear to be the same as a small keel and with the same disadvantages, the intent is to provide more stability in a boat rolled up on its side (heeled over).

This is done by flaring the sides of the hull and making the bottom less flat or even forming it into a slight V at the keel line. When the boat is heeled over, more hull surface remains in the water, thus providing a more stable platform for the whole boat.

There is one other factor in hull design that I feel obligated to mention, as it is of great concern to many canoeists. This is "sheer"

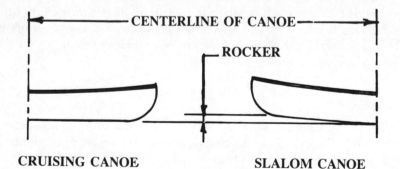

CRUISING CANOE   SLALOM CANOE

ROCKER IN A HULL

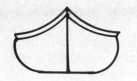 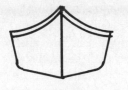

"STANDARD" HULL   **"FLARED" HULL WITH V   BOTTOM**

BOTTOM AND HULL SHAPES

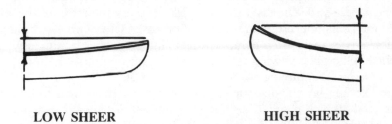

LOW SHEER   **HIGH SHEER**

height, the amount the bow and stern rise above the gunwales at the midpoint of the hull. There are two schools of thought. One says that a high sheer may catch wind on a windy day but cuts through waves better, ergo less water in the boat. The other school says a lower sheer doesn't catch as much wind and keeps the water out just as well. Who's right? I have no idea. Personally, I prefer the high sheer because it looks more like a canoe to me, but the tendency seems to be toward low sheer designs.

Other Design Factors

There are many other subtleties of design, of course, but most are too esoteric to worry about unless you plan to become a professional. Most of us couldn't tell the difference anyway. The point is, enjoy the boat you have or can get—you can become more high-tech later.

Keels

A canoe with no keel makes a better river solo boat than one with a keel. While a keeled boat can certainly be handled solo, the smaller the keel is, the easier the boat is to maneuver. A smooth hull section, one with no keel at all, offers the maximum response. There is a good reason for this. Most river maneuvers involve quick-turning movements (pivots) or movements to the side. Anything protruding from the bottom of the hull (such as a keel) offers a decided resistance to such lateral motion. So it is nice not to have a keel on your solo boat. Nice but not absolutely necessary, not at first anyway.

There are only two main types of keel, and both have several names: the lake, cruising, T, or full, for one; and the shoe, river, or whitewater keel for the other. Most are shaped about as shown in the drawing, varying only in size. Both run down the center of the flat part of the bottom of the hull and terminate where the bow and stern begin.

Cruising keels make a canoe "track" better – follow the linear path the paddle stroke sends it in – and resist the yawing effect of the wind. These keels, therefore, are intended to resist lateral changes in direction. River keels are a compromise. They give less tracking ability to the hull and less yawing resistance. They are obviously better choices if you insist on buying a hull with a keel on it.

No keel at all, of course, offers the least resistance to sideways motion – which is great for maneuvering but not always so wonderful other times. Paddling a keelless solo boat in a given straight line path on a windy day, in fact, is a real test of both ability and equanimity, as the usual lightly loaded boat wants to blow all over the river simply because it has nothing to resist these unwanted side motions. At such times, solo paddlers can only grit their teeth, dig in, and take comfort from the thought that when the necessity does once more arise for quick maneuvers, they will be ready. But remember, both keeled and keelless boats can be paddled solo, it's just that one won't be as easy to maneuver. If you have a boat with a keel, use it; you can worry about something more suitable later.

| CRUISING, | WHITEWATER , | NONE |
| LAKE, T | SHOE, RIVER | |

BASIC KEEL TYPES

Materials

Ah, material! Our modern age has wreaked havoc with the old wood-and-canvas and aluminum hulls – or at least with the idea of their being perfect canoe materials!

There are currently about five basic canoe hull materials to choose from: wood, aluminum, fiberglass, Kevlar, and ABS. Of these, the last three, the "plastics" group of technological progress, are the most common (and most suitable) for solo usage.

Wood and aluminum hulls can be used, of course, but the rough and tumble usage of most solo boating, certain manufacturing considerations (plastic can be formed into shapes difficult or impossible to achieve with wood or metal), and such factors as maintenance and difficulty of repair inevitably lead most solo boaters away from these traditional materials.

Two of the plastics – fiberglass and Kevlar – are cloth impregnated with resin. The type of cloth and its weight, the number and placing of the layers, and the particular blend of resin used vary with the intended use of the boat and the manufacturer's ideas, research, and whims. In the same design hull an all-Kevlar layup, for example, can be strong and lightweight; a fiberglass and Kevlar mix (in layers) usually creates a heavier but still strong and relatively lightweight boat; and an all fiberglass layup will probably be the heaviest for the same strength. Exotic variations such as E glass and S glass, graphite fibers, and different resins add varying degrees of strength, flexibility, or impact resistance to the hull.

Hulls of Kevlar or fiberglass or combinations thereof are quiet, flexible, fairly strong, and lightweight if built by hand layup methods. They are also easy to repair if damaged. Do beware of fiberglass boats built by the chopped mat method (sprayed in a mold as are many power boats) or built of roving, a heavy fiberglass resembling burlap in texture. These are weaker and heavier boats compared to other methods of production. Both usually betray their presence by the rough textured look of the interior of the hull and, often, by the low price of the boat!

The other plastic – ABS – is a composite. ABS stands for acrilan-butadiene-styrene, which is of no importance whatsoever. What is important is that many paddlers consider it to be the best material available for a canoe. ABS hulls are flexible, slippery, quiet, extremely tough, and no heavier than any other canoe of comparable size. They are also easy to patch. The heart of an ABS hull is an expanded foam core. This is covered with layers of ABS plastic and topped off with a vinyl layer. Various manufacturers use varying layups and apply extra

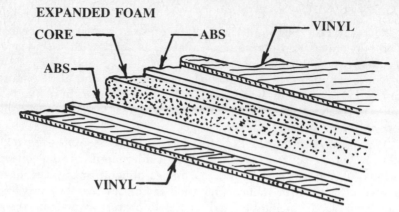

EXPANDED FOAM
CORE ——   ——**ABS**   ——**VINYL**

ABS—

VINYL—

TYPICAL ABS FOAM CORE LAYUP

layers at strategic points, but the basic material for all ABS hulls is the same. Pure ABS hulls – those *not* of foam-core construction – are tough, but are usually too flexible, too hard to patch, and often too poorly designed, to be considered for river use.

Any of the plastics make good canoes, provided they are built by a reputable manufacturer or a reputable individual. Foam-core ABS is probably the best all-around choice for a solo boat, however.

And So?

In light of all this, then, there are two big basic classes of canoe normally used for open, solo river canoeing: the "standard" boats and those intended strictly for solo slalom use. Between this alpha and omega are an infinite number of degrees of suitability, and only you can define this rather vague criteria. It is your choice, your decision, and your money.

I strongly suggest you start wherever you are and end where you will. If solo paddling becomes your thing, you will probably not rest with whatever boat you start with, but will progress through a string of ever-hotter designs until you find "your" boat – or meet your match!

2

Canoe Modifications

Almost any canoe suitable for solo use (in terms of length, width, etc.) can be satisfactorily paddled just as it comes from the dealer. There are, however, various ways to modify your canoe for better solo use. How much modification you decide to do depends on several things, the major two being whether you intend to use the canoe exclusively for solo, or to also paddle it tandem; and the roughness of the water you intend to tackle.

Canoe modifications usually fall into three categories: adding flotation to keep the water out and thus reducing the likelihood of swamping; adding knee straps, solo saddles, etc. to brace the paddler in and make the boat more responsive to paddler body movements; and shifting its pivot point to improve the boat's maneuverability. You may want to do any or all of these. Some are simple and easily added, changed, or removed; some are not. Whatever you elect to do, think it out in the light of future paddling activities as well as coordination with other changes. Relocating a thwart, for example, affects bracing location. Most canoeists will probably want to strike some medium that will leave the boat suitable for several uses without complicated remodifications for each one.

Improving Maneuverability

Shift the Pivot Point

This is the basic and easiest way to make your boat more maneuverable. It's done by simply shifting your paddling position to near the
center of the length of the hull. Remember that a canoe hull tends to
pivot around its deepest point in the water. Commonly, this point is
where the paddler's weight is, so by moving your weight you also
move the pivot point. This immediately reduces the turning radius of
the boat by nearly half its length.

This weight shift also balances the boat better and reduces the
weight on bow and stern so they have less tendency to dig into waves.
In addition, paddling becomes easier in some cases because the turning effect of some paddle strokes is decreased by this mid-hull position, yet you can reach out in both directions and apply your paddle
action to the front or rear of the hull when you do want a turning or
diagonal effect. Also, the power of side strokes such as draws and pries
is more evenly applied to the length of the hull instead of creating a
turning movement as they would when done at the end of the hull.

Relocate the Thwarts

While moving toward the center of the boat can result in better
control and maneuverability, it does little good to move if you can't
stay there, and you can't stay there without something to brace on.
This is where your first real modification comes in. The easiest way to
provide a brace behind you is to add or relocate a thwart so it provides
the third point of your "three-point kneeling position." Thwart loca-

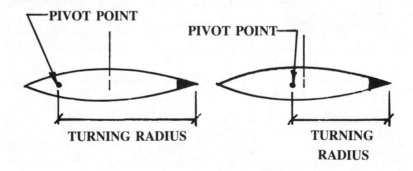

PIVOT POINTS

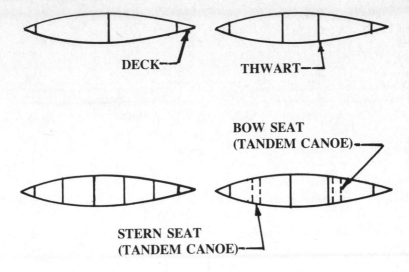

DECK—◥   THWART—◥

BOW SEAT
(TANDEM CANOE)—◥

STERN SEAT
(TANDEM CANOE)—◥

SOME TYPICAL "FACTORY" THWART LOCATIONS

tions vary depending on the manufacturer, the hull length, and the boat's intended use. Many pure solo boats come with a thwart or "seat" (actually a wide thwart) already in the correct location, others with an unattached thwart for you to install. Your boat may already have a suitably located thwart (or one close enough), or you may find that turning the boat around and paddling it stern first puts a thwart in a better location for you.

Where is this more suitable location? Mostly that's a matter of feel and judgment. As far as height above the bottom of the hull, many factory thwarts are gunwale high. Although a final decision on this depends on the depth of your canoe and your own height, gunwale-high thwarts usually prove to be too high. They force unaccustomed weight on your knees, and more important, they raise your center of gravity too far.

Experiment to find a comfortable and stable height, then adjust the vertical location of the thwart with strong wood or metal braces firmly attached in the same manner as the original thwart. If your thwart is flat, like a board (as in many solo canoes), you may also want to angle it, low side toward the bow, for a more comfortable position. Never lower a thwart so much that you create a hazard of foot entrapment under it.

For longitudinal thwart position, the majority of solo paddlers

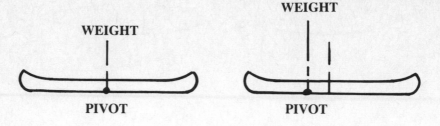

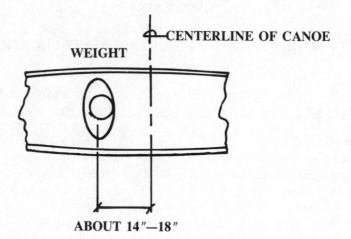

SOLO PADDLER LOCATION

seem to like a position with their knees about on the centerline of the hull. As this puts most of the body weight about 14 to 18 inches behind the centerline, it trims the boat in the slightly bow-high position that seems to be favored. The final location, of course, will depend on your physical size, your usual kneeling stance, and, in the case of an extra thwart, how claustrophobic you get about your legs being in between two of them.

Depending upon your original thwart location, you may need to remove and relocate one or more, or install a new one. To remove riveted thwarts, drill out the old rivets with a bit a little smaller than the rivet shaft, then cut off the head and punch the rivet out. For a do-it-yourself wood or metal thwart, use straight-grained spruce or maple or round or oval aluminum tubing. Thwarts can have a lot of pressure on them, so be careful of the alloy and wall thickness of any tubing you buy. Matching that already on your canoe is a good idea for strength as well as looks.

Determine the length and location by trial and error; kneel in the boat and move the thwart around until it suits you. Be sure to leave enough space so the new and old thwarts don't become leg trappers. Cut the thwart to fit, modify the ends to suit whatever mounting method is used in your boat, make or buy any mounting brackets needed, and drill your holes. The better fit you have in all this, the stronger the new thwart will be.

Machine screw or rivet the assembly in place. Pop or cherry rivets are the easiest. If you use screws and want a fairly permanent installation, use fiber locknuts and plain washers. For an easily removable thwart, use wing nuts and lock washers. Obviously, all nuts and screw ends should be down, not up.

Keeping The Water Out – Flotation

Extra flotation is the next most common and easy modification to a canoe. It's also excellent insurance that does just one thing: reduces the amount of water that can be in the hull, whether that water be from rain, splash, or total submersion. This fundamental task, however, serves three very important purposes:

1. Lessens the probability of the boat becoming uncontrollable or sinking because of excess water in the hull.

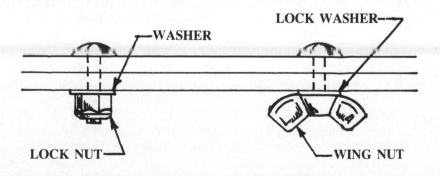

2. Reduces the chances of pinning and damage to the boat if it is swamped, because the hull will be much lighter and ride higher without all that water in it.
3. Facilitates rescue of the canoe because it is riding higher and is lighter.

A side benefit is that strategically placed flotation of the right type can also be used as a leg brace or even a saddle for the paddler.

The only disadvantages are the additional weight the flotation adds, the difficulty of one person carrying the canoe (the flotation often either unbalances the boat or physically gets in the way), and the reduced storage space in the hull for the trip's supplies. All these disadvantages, however, are very minor when compared to benefits.

Although any flotation in a canoe helps, the more that's in the boat, the less room there is for water, so many solo paddlers cram the hull full of it except for their kneeling space. Ultimately, however, how much and where depends upon what kind of water you're tackling and whether the boat is to be set up for tandem or strictly solo. I've seen bags of ping-pong balls, children's rubber balls, and other homey items used for flotation, but the three most common (and more effective) types are inner tubes, foam blocks, and air bags. Each has its advantages and disadvantages.

Inner Tubes

Inner tubes are tough, cheap, readily available, easily installed and removed, and easily patched; they also provide a neat round space in the middle to store a day's supplies. On the other hand, they are heavy for their volume and displace less water than other methods because they can't be made to fit the hull as well, no matter how cleverly stuffed into it.

Typically a solo paddler will install a tube in bow and stern. What size is used depends on the space available, but fewer large tubes are preferable to more smaller ones. Installation is simple; partially inflate the tubes and squeeze them into the bow and stern or wherever, forcing them under any available seat or thwart. Large tubes usually have long, angled valve stems that are safest for you if pointed down toward the bottom of the hull. Inflate the tubes more fully once they're in position, but not too tightly as this makes them more subject to puncture.

Secure the tubes in the boat. Stern tubes can usually be wedged under and tied off to stern seats or thwarts. Bow tubes usually require some sort of cross lacing to hold them. One simple and efficient way is to drill holes in your gunwales or hull and lace synthetic rope through the holes. Drill the holes only just large enough for the rope. Used in conjunction with a longitudinal strap attached to glued-down D rings on the bottom of the hull; this method virtually guarantees your bags staying *put*! Some manufacturers offer such strap, D ring, and adhesive pad kits just for this purpose. Another way is to put small eye bolts in your gunwales. Still another method, a more permanent one, is to install D rings at strategic locations on the inside of the hull. Glue, rivet, or fiberglass them in (depending on your hull material), then lace through the rings. The D ring sets made for knee straps work well for this. Still another way is to pop rivet the "speed" lace rings used on boots (available in shoe repair shops) to the inside of the gunwales and lace through them. Probably the least strong but easiest method is to add short eye screws to the inside of your gunwales. Depending on your gunwale material, you may need to drill pilot holes for the screws. Use nylon or some other synthetic cord for all the lacing; ⅛ inch is a good size.

Inner tube flotation held in place by a part of the canoe.

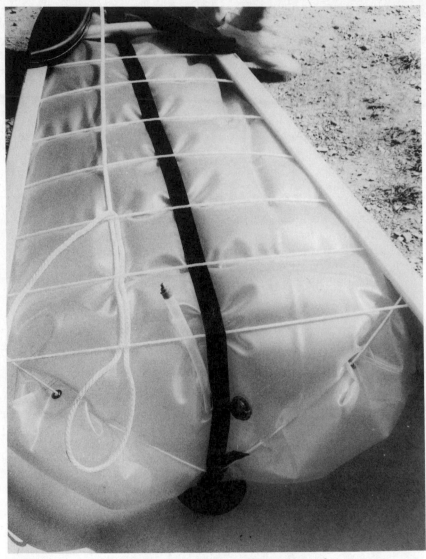

Air bags secured by both lacing and a D ring and strap.

Air Bags

Air bags are perhaps the most satisfactory extra flotation. Because they are form fit, they fill up the hull more completely than inner tubes and are lighter in weight for their volume. They are relatively easy to install and remove, are generally available, and easily patched.

Air bags are usually of heavy vinyl (20 mil is common) and of one-piece, heat-sealed construction. Most of them have two air valves, a large one for major inflation and rapid deflation, and a smaller one usually on the end of a flexible tube for final inflation on the installed bag and for "topping" up the bag at other times. The bags are available in various shapes and sizes, but in general they are either rectangular for mid-hull installation or triangular for bow and stern use. They are built specifically for kayaks, decked canoes, or open canoes, but obviously they can be switched from one type of boat to another if they fit. A set of triangular bags for a solo boat typically weighs about six to seven pounds.

Holes drilled in the gunwale hold this air-bag lacing.

Air bags are installed the same as tubes – partially inflated, positioned, then fully inflated. The small "topping" valve should be up to be accessible. Although most of the bags have some built-in grommets for tying them in, cross-lacing such as described for tubes is definitely recommended and is usually necessary in the case of the bow bag.

Foam Blocks

Foam blocks (usually styrofoam) are light, easily worked with a sharp knife or saw, can be made almost as form fitting as your patience allows, are strong in large block size, and are obviously not susceptible to puncturing. Large blocks are sometimes hard to find, however, and installation is more troublesome than either tubes or bags. Some paddlers pack the entire hull with foam, leaving only room for their kneeling area; others extend it into or through the kneeling area and make a saddle of that part of it. Still others install only a single bow and stern block.

The tops of foam blocks usually stop even with the gunwale or extend a few inches above it. To install the foam, remove the seats and thwarts where the foam will be, fit the foam to the hull, "spring" the hull apart, put the foam in under the gunwales, then replace the seats and thwarts, fitting them into notches cut in the top of the foam if necessary. If you don't want to go to this trouble, just let the pressure of the seat or thwart hold the somewhat resilient foam in place with a tight fit. You'll still have to remove the seats or thwarts to install it, however.

Replace the original seat and thwart fasteners (rivets or screws) with wing nuts and lock washers if you intend to remove the foam very often. Cut out notches in the foam at their locations so you can get to the wing nuts. One point: when you're fitting foam to the hull, avoid creating any thin sections in the foam. They will be brittle and weak and probably won't last long. If large foam blocks are unobtainable, smaller blocks can either be fitted together and held in place by the canoe parts, or glued together with a hot-melt glue gun.

Decks/Spray Covers

Decks or spray covers on solo canoes furnish no extra flotation and do no good once the boat is swamped. They do, however, keep out some water from splash, rain, and a little gunwale dipping. There are a few commercially made spray covers available, usually for a specific canoe. These may have one, two, or three cockpits. Many paddlers, however, prefer to custom build one to suit their own boat. Most paddlers cover the whole hull, except for a cockpit; others fully deck the bow and partially deck the stern. On fully covered boats, the cockpit is usually built with a ring or rim so a standard decked canoe or kayak spray skirt can be used.

Covers are usually made of coated canvas or urethane-coated nylon in a fairly heavy weight. The most common method of attachment to the hull is with snap fasteners, the male section pop riveted to the hull a few inches below the gunwale and the female part on the edge of the cover. Twist fasteners such as used on sports car tops and covers work very well, but they are usually rather large, hard to install, and somewhat expensive.

Another method is to use grommetted holes in the cover and small eye bolts in the hull. A nylon rope is then laced through the holes and the eye bolts. A variation is elastic cord, sewn in the deck material, then hooked through open eye bolts or cup hooks in the hull. In both of these methods, the eye bolts are likely to get bent and the open bolts are somewhat dangerous.

Two additions are often made to spray covers. Covers do need to be taut and wrinkle free to shed water, so some sort of light support under the cover is usually needed to give it a convex, water-shedding shape and to provide support when water crashes down on it. This is often as simple as a strong, small-diameter rope run down the middle of the hull from the bow and stern to the thwarts just in front of and behind the paddler. The other addition is a tiedown or two on each side of the hull near the bow. This holds the cover in place when the boat noses down and water pushes up on it. Painters extend through small grommetted holes at the bow and stern, and loops or some sort of tiedown are usually sewed to the outside of the cover to hold an extra paddle.

Easy, trap-free exit is of great interest to the solo paddler. Whatever spray cover or deck you buy or create should use a standard C1 or K1 spray skirt that detaches by simply "popping" the elastic cord that holds it to the cockpit. *Do not* use or build one that you drawstring around your waist; this effectively ties you in the boat — not a desirable situation when the boat rolls over!

Bracing the Paddler

The idea of bracing the paddler in position in solo canoeing is to increase control. You must be stable in the boat. If you're sliding all over the hull, you can't control the paddle or use your weight and

muscle very well. Another advantage is transferring your body movements to the hull, creating a single unit of boat and paddler. This adds
greatly to both confidence and maneuverability. There are several
common ways of increasing your stability, holding you in position and
yet letting you lean and move to your advantage rather than ignomini-
ously falling out of the boat.

Knee Pads

Wearing common old knee pads helps a lot. The "on-the-leg" type
are discussed in more detail in the next chapter, so let me simply say
here that most of them have some sort of "tire tread" on the bottom that
grips the hull of the boat with enough friction to eliminate nearly all
the sliding of the knees.

Knee pads come in a variety of shapes, sizes, and thicknesses.
Avoid those of sponge rubber or any open-cell foam; although soft,
they hold water, and worse, they hold grit and sand—guaranteed to
give you a case of sandpapered knees in no time at all. Two straps on
the pads won't work into an uncomfortable wad behind your knee

Locate glued-in knee pads to suit your usual paddling position.

as badly as one-strap pads or wide elastic straps. Personally, I prefer the thin, black, molded-rubber type sold for gardening or concrete finishing.

Built-in Knee Pads

Some canoeists prefer to attach their knee pads to the hull of the canoe instead of to their legs. This is usually done by gluing the individual pads down with contact cement. Remove the straps; *you* don't want to be glued to your canoe! A more practical method and one that allows better movement is to glue a single wide pad or two smaller pads to the hull at the kneeling location. This is usually closed-cell foam that doesn't absorb water or degrade too badly in the sun. Volara-foam is one common type, Neoprene is another. They are available from several manufacturers or you can create your own.

Thigh Straps

Thigh straps serve as a brace in front of you, holding you securely between them and the thwart behind you. Unlike knee pads, which only stop skidding in the hull, properly adjusted thigh straps lock you into the boat so your movements become the boat's movements. De-

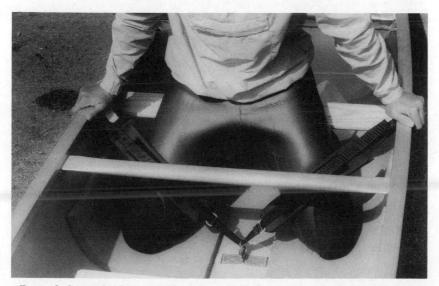

Properly located thigh straps brace you in the canoe, but don't trap you in it.

spite their name, they do not literally strap you in; to free yourself, simply relax the pressure on your legs.

Thigh straps are generally of nylon laced through D rings attached to the hull of the canoe by riveting, gluing, or fiberglassing, depending on the hull material. Although you can make your own, it's usually easier to buy a kit and install it. Obviously, the location of the straps is very important, and has to be determined by positioning yourself in the boat. The straps are adjustable for tightness and should be located so they firmly hold you when you want them to, yet will not hold you or entangle your legs when you abruptly exit the boat.

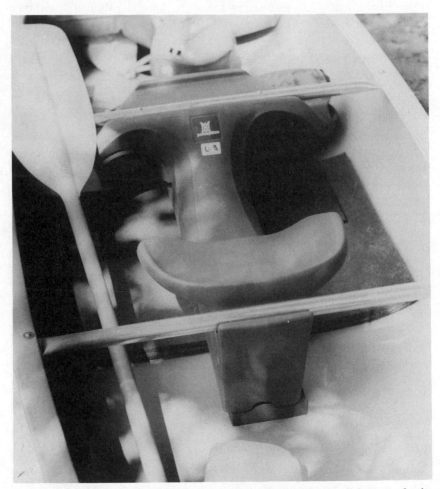

A commercial solo saddle. This one is blocked up with closed-cell foam under it.

Solo Saddles

Solo "saddles" give you a firm seat in the boat, a brace behind you, and, with some saddles, a knee brace in front of you. You can also grip the saddle between your thighs. The overall result is a nice, stable, comfortable, and secure cockpit arrangement. You can create your own saddle out of block foam or buy one ready-made. Many paddlers using foam blocks for flotation extend the foam on through the cockpit area and trim it out to a suitable "saddle" shape. You could also have only a block saddle notched under the thwarts in a boat filled with air bags. Any home-built saddle, obviously, will be a product of cut and fit and try and trim until it seats you at the location and height you want and fits your own taste and derrière.

Factory saddles are molded devices usually with premolded notches that fit under the thwarts behind and in front of the paddler. You may need to move a thwart to fit the notches unless the saddle is made for your boat. The single disadvantage of a factory saddle is that it's a general design and may not quite fit you. You may need to build it up a little or do some reshaping with foam on the seat portion or block

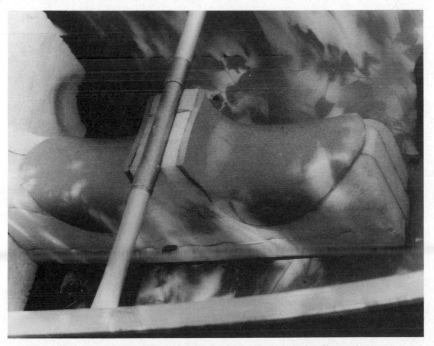

A homemade saddle of styrofoam with a closed-cell topping.

Bang plates save a lot of wear and tear on both bow and stern.

it up underneath to raise it to the height you want. If you do any of these, remember that thin pieces of styrofoam break and chip easily, so use a more rubbery textured foam.

Foot Braces

Foot braces make paddling easier by allowing you to apply more of your body weight and strength. With block flotation you may already have something to brace against, or you can buy or make your own braces. Some kits are available for canoes, are complete with mounting attachments, or you can adapt kayak foot braces. Another expedient is to make a bar of aluminum tubing or channel (or some strong wood if you prefer), mount it on wooden blocks to bring it up to the right height for your feet, and epoxy or rivet it to the hull.

Skid (Bang) Plates

These are not strictly for solo use, but they are a good idea on a solo canoe. Made of Kevlar, the plates fit on bow and stern and extend back along the keel line past the "bend" of the bow and stern. They absorb a lot of the punishment the hull would otherwise receive from banging into rocks and the like. Skid plates are glued (epoxied) on with resin usually supplied with the kit in which they come. Obviously you could also make your own.

3

Paddles, Pads, and Appurtenances

Although a canoe is essential to solo canoeing, it's only one part of the story. Other items are also needed. Some are necessary, some are for comfort, convenience, or safety; all will help you wend your solitary way down the river.

Paddles

It's very difficult to canoe without a paddle. As this is the tool that translates your thoughts and actions into canoe movements, its selection deserves more than a little thought. A comfortable, effective, sturdy paddle is the ultimate goal. The paddle is what you do the actual work of paddling with. Although the efficiency of that work is very dependent on your paddling technique, the paddle itself can affect that efficiency, and how much work or wasted effort you expend on those river miles.

Numerous factors enter into the selection of a paddle, some objective and some subjective. Material, grip style, blade width, overall length, and weight are objective. "Spring," balance, and appearance are

37

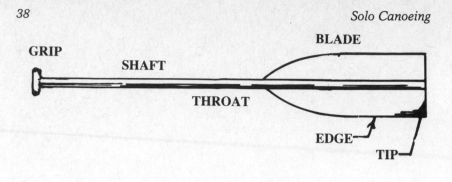

PARTS OF A PADDLE

subjective. All are subject to your personal whims, fancies, and bank account.

Sturdy material is essential! River running is rough on paddles. Contact with rocks is common, jamming blades between underwater obstructions happens all the time, the stresses and strains created by maneuvers are severe, and general mistreatment takes its toll. Wood, aluminum, or epoxy shafts, ABS, Kevlar, wood, or fiberglass blades are all common materials. All are good, but many paddlers feel that, in paddles of equal quality, wooden shafts and blades—though beautiful, light, springy, and relatively strong—are not as well suited for continued hard river usage as the other materials.

Shafts should be strong—a compromise between the requirements of strength and light weight. Shafts should also be a good size. Too small a shaft is hard to grip and control, too large a diameter feels equally uncomfortable. The size of the shaft also aids your sense of security; you'll have more faith in a sturdy-feeling shaft and paddle. Blades may be rigid or have some flex to them. This is a matter of choice. Very flexible blades are likely to break; they also "give" too much for good canoe control. Rigid blades, however, feel uncomfortable to some paddlers and do not give that little kick to the end of a paddle stroke. Generally, solo paddlers tend toward stiffer blades and shafts.

Blade width is important but again, a matter of personal choice. Too narrow a blade won't get the work done and makes braces positively hazardous, but too wide a blade works you to death. Generally a width of about 7½ to 8 inches is a good choice to start with. This will give you good thrust and help quick direction changes. There are a lot of blade and tip shapes to choose from and I'm sure each one has good reasons for being that shape—but I don't know what they are. What I

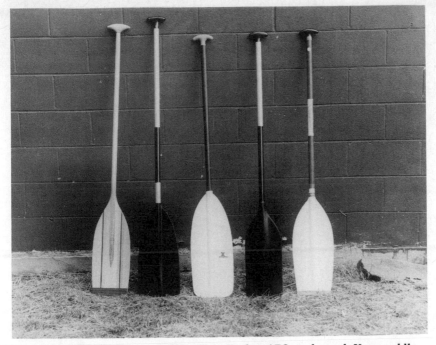

Typical paddles are of wood, fiberglass, Kevlar, ABS, and wood. Your paddle—your choice.

do know is that square tips give more blade surface area than other shapes on the same size blade and that long, deep blades are more able to catch the "solid" water below the aerated surface water found in rapids. You can take it from there.

The strongest paddles have the shaft extended on down into the blade, often all the way to the tip. Some paddles also have metal tip reinforcement built in; nearly all paddles are reinforced in some way at the tip. Grip shape is important. The grip needs to be comfortable, shaped for a good grip, and large enough to hold firmly. This is important both for paddle control and for simply hanging on to the paddle when strain is on it. The T grip is a very popular choice.

Overall paddle weight varies with length, material, and design. Too heavy a paddle adds up to a lot of extra work over the course of a day; too light a paddle is likely to be fragile. Currently most good quality paddles range from about 2½ to 3½ pounds. Comparing brands or borrowing different paddles is a good way to determine this very relative "light-heavy" question.

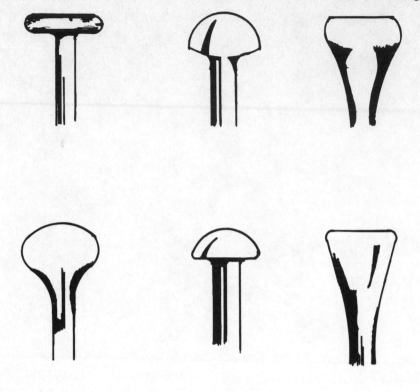

SOME VARIOUS PADDLE GRIPS

In terms of length, your paddle must fit you. One too long or too short will severely hamper your paddling efforts. Although there are all sorts of ideas on proper paddle length, a good average starting length for most people is the distance from the ground to somewhere between their chin and nose. Experience will show you if you want one longer or shorter. Custom paddles are built to your specified length, but many commercial paddles are only available in about six-inch multiples. So you may not be able to fit your paddle into this chin/ground length. In this case, get the longer paddle; many solo paddlers prefer one slightly longer than they would use in a tandem canoe.

Bent-shaft paddles are available. The blade is cocked off at an angle to the shaft so that in normal paddling the blade force stays perpendicular in the water longer, giving you a much more efficient paddle stroke. On the other hand, they reduce your reach somewhat and must be oriented for correct usage. In general, canoeists interested in cruising seem to like the bent-shaft design, those more interested in maneuvering prefer the standard straight-shaft configuration.

Avoid paddles held together with screws and slip-fits. Solid assemblies are much stronger. The advantage of being able to replace a broken or lost blade or grip is negligible when compared to strength.

Ground to nose or chin: one way to determine a good beginning-length paddle.

Spring, balance, appearance, and feel are subjective qualities that only you can determine. Spring is the "give" of a paddle when it's used. Some like it, some don't. Wooden paddles generally have a lot of spring, fiberglass ones very little. Balance and feel are totally intangible. Does the paddle "feel" right when you hold it and use it? If it doesn't, after you've used it a while, it's probably going to affect your paddling. After all, your paddle stays in your hands most of the time on a canoe trip, so you need to feel at home with it. Appearance? Another intangible, but important to some for its aid to the feeling of being at home with the paddle.

When buying a paddle, your best bet is to stick to well-known brands that are in popular usage among river canoeists. You'll probably get as many opinions on paddles as canoeists you ask, but if the paddlers are experienced, they won't lead you too far astray. You can then narrow the choices down and make your own selection. You'll probably change your mind later anyway as your experience increases!

Life Jackets

Dignified by the name *personal flotation device* (PFD), life jackets are generally legally required in all canoes and should be there even if not required. Buy only Coast Guard–approved devices, because they are the only ones accepted by the various water patrols, conservation departments, and other regulatory offices. Homemade (kit) PFDs are not Coast Guard–approved although they may be as good as or maybe better than some approved designs.

The Coast Guard divides PFDs into five types. Type 4 PFDs are throwing devices such as seat cushions and rings, and should never be used in canoeing. Type 1 and Type 5 devices are bulky and heavy and usually reserved for extremely heavy water in rafts or decked boats. Types 2 and 3 PFDs are the choice then for solo canoeing. Type 2 devices add a greater amount of flotation and are intended to turn an unconscious person face up in the water (not infallible; there are too many variables in the human body for it to always work); they are probably the best and safest PFD for canoeing. However, the less bulky Type 3 jackets, which have less required additional flotation and are not designed to turn an unconscious person face upward, are more popular, more in use, and more comfortable, and are perfectly suitable for most rivers.

PFDs come in various weight ranges and sizes. In most jackets the amount of extra flotation increases with size, beginning with the

A plethora of PFDs, but all Type 3 jackets.

minimum required flotation in the smallest size. In others, however, the flotation remains fairly constant regardless of size. Jacket styles are preferable to the "horse-collar" type. Jackets are warmer in cold weather, give more impact protection, are generally more comfortable, and are less likely to be ripped from your body. Jackets should fit snugly but comfortably and be adjustable to your body. Arm holes and neck openings should be large enough to allow freedom of movement and not chafe your armpits or neck (very irritating in the summer).

Most PFDs are filled with foam, either many narrow strips or fewer, wider strips. In general, the narrow strip types mold to the body better and are more comfortable. Outer coverings come in a variety of materials, colors, and patterns, with assorted pockets and doodads, none of which makes much difference except to the style-conscious paddler!

Your PFD does no good tied or zipped around a thwart out of reach. Use it! Wear it all the time if you can't swim or if it's winter. Otherwise, put it on well *before* you think you'll need it. If it's not on your body, keep it handy. I could say some words about mistreating your PFD, but I won't; we all use them for seats and backrests at one time or another.

Helmets

There was a time when helmets were not worn by paddlers except on the heaviest of waters. Now their use is required on many rivers or sections of rivers. There is no doubt that open-boat paddlers should unfailingly wear them on Class 3 water, and many safety-conscious boaters strap them on in Class 2 rapids. They are good insurance and excellent protection against a head injury. Helmets are worn to provide protection to the skull and temple from impact, crushing, and penetration by objects in the river. There are no standards for white-water helmets as of this writing, but there are various opinions as to what is best.

In general, a fairly heavy, rigid helmet lined with crushable foam and cut to provide good temple protection is considered safest; the

This helmet has already saved the paddler's skull from some licks.

same helmet with resilient foam next best; and a helmet with a sling suspension support, third. Flexible, lightweight helmets with many large drain holes are usually not too safe.

Many factors enter into helmet selection: comfort, weight, price, availability, and the degree of protection wanted. All are a matter of personal choice. Helmets are generally constructed of ABS, fiberglass, or Kevlar. Some are of the "poly" plastics. Crushable foam, resilient foam, or a sling suspension system either with or without crown and/or temple pads are the usual linings or supports.

Many helmets have drain holes to allow water to run out, although this is not considered essential. Drain holes may even reduce the protection. Some have bills for glare reduction, but they may create buffeting effects if the paddler is in the water. Some helmets cover all or part of the ears and/or temples, others only one or the other; some even cover noses. Adjustable chin straps may be nylon or other fabric, with fasteners, buckles, or D rings as the helmet retainer. D rings are considered the best and most secure. Many helmets with sling suspensions are one size only, with all adjustments for fit made in the sling system. Others are available in various sizes. Fully foam-lined helmets fall in this last category.

Throw Ropes and Bags

Throw ropes and bags are rescue and safety devices. One or more should be along on every trip. They are thrown to swimming or stranded paddlers to get them to shore, but they're also extremely useful in rescuing pinned boats, as safety lines, and even to hang up river-wet clothing. A throw rope is simply a rope coiled in a certain way so it uncoils smoothly when thrown. It has to be recoiled for each throw. A throw bag is a similar rope that's stuffed down into a bag, with one end of the rope attached to the inside of the bag in some manner. A throw-bag rope does not have to be recoiled each time. It's simply slung and the weight of the wet bag pulls it out. It takes less skill and usually slightly less time than a throw rope to make a good first throw.

Both ropes are usually 50 to 60 feet long (shorter is not too useful and longer is hard to handle) and about $7/16$ to $5/8$ inch in diameter. Too small a rope is hard for the victim to grasp, as well as the rescuer to throw, and too large a diameter is bulky and difficult to handle. The ropes are normally a bright, easily seen color and a synthetic material such as polypropylene or nylon. They may or may not be floatable.

Some canoeists advocate knots or loops tied in the ends of a throw

A throw rope or throw bag is essential safety equipment.

rope for the victim to grasp. Others consider any protruberance on a rope more likely to snag, thus not worth any value they may have.

Although throw bags might seem to have all the advantages (quick throw, no coiling, little required skill except for aiming), the usual preference seems to be throw bags for the recreational paddler and throw ropes for the professional guide. Several reasons may account for this: the bag of a throw bag may snag on something in the river, rendering the rope useless until it's freed; the pulled-in and dropped rope of a throw bag may tie itself in knots when hastily thrown a second time; and, with practice, a throw rope is almost as fast for a second throw.

Throw bags can be bought or made; throw ropes are bought. Be sure to burn (fuse) the ends of any synthetic rope together to stop raveling or unweaving and to "whip" the ends of a natural-fiber rope for the same reason.

Keep throw ropes and bags neatly and securely tied in the boat, out of the way but ready and available for action. Look in the appendix of this book for directions on throwing both bags and ropes.

Knee Pads

Most of your solo canoeing will be done on your knees, and bare knees were not made to kneel on all day—they get sore, tired, and uncomfortable. Even with a saddle, there's still weight and pressure on the patellas, and paddling can make you acutely aware of this until you get used to it. Knee pads are the usual answer, either removable ones you put on or pads built into your canoe. Apart from knee protection, knee pads also help keep you braced in the canoe by providing some traction between your knees and the hull—a decidedly better arrangement than kneeling on something loose, such as a life jacket, that lets you slide around everytime it does.

Removable knee pads are commonly of molded rubber or foam-filled cloth bags. Most of the molded rubber types have adjustable straps with buckles, although some slip on. The others (athletic-type knee protectors) usually have a slip-on wide elastic band. Molded rubber pads with a single strap and cloth pads with elastic straps often end up with the strap right in the bend of the leg when you're kneel-

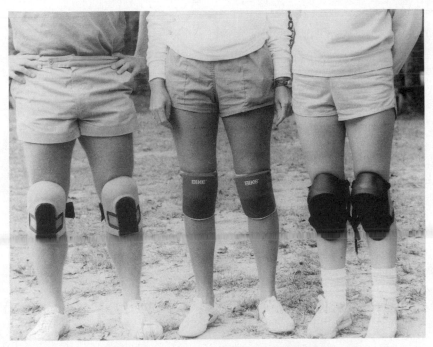

Three of many types of knee pads available.

ing – that's uncomfortable and tends to cut off the blood circulation. Pads with two or more straps usually don't have this problem.

Molded-rubber pads quickly drain and dry, and some have a thick closed-cell foam cushion in them. Some are even comfortable. Most have "treads" of some kind to grip the canoe hull better. Foam-filled pads stay wet longer and seem to trap sand and grit, a source of irritation both to the paddler and his "sandpapered" knees. Some paddlers, however, seem to have no problem with this. It's all a matter of choice, but you do need pads of some kind.

Transporting the Canoe

Getting your canoe to and from the river involves carrying it on something other than your back. Trailers are sometimes used, but the average solo canoeist transports it on top of a personal vehicle.

Secure and sturdy racks on which the boat or boats rest, cross tiedowns to hold the boat to the racks, and painters to hold it to the vehicle against the pressures of the wind and driving movements are the three requirements of safe, successful transportation.

Painters

Painters are the ropes on the bow and stern of a canoe. They stay on the boat and are used primarily to tie the canoe down to the vehicle and secondarily to secure the canoe to something while you're on a trip.

Painters need to be long enough to allow the boat to be tied down when it's on its usual racks, yet not have a lot of loose rope left over. The overall length will vary with the vehicle; canoes carried on the top of pickup trucks or vans will probably need longer painters than those carried on passenger cars. A length of 10 to 12 feet will usually do. Remember, however, the boat may sometime be shuttled on some larger vehicle than yours and need slightly longer painters than you would normally install. Too long a painter is troublesome; so is one too short.

Painters should be ¼ to ⅜ inch in diameter; anything larger is totally unnecessary. The rope only needs to be strong enough to hold the boat down against wind load when you're traveling. Nylon or polypropylene rope is a good choice. Keep the ends of these synthetics from fraying or unraveling by burning them; "whip" the ends of natural fibers. When paddling, coil the painter up in the end of the hull and tie it or stuff it in behind your flotation. Don't leave it trailing in the

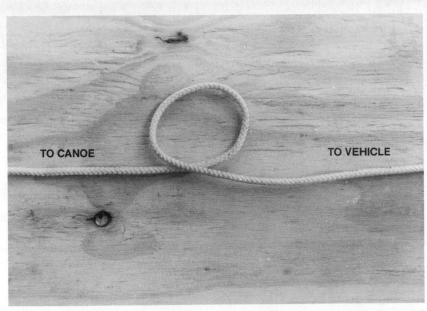

TO CANOE   TO VEHICLE

Make an initial loop. The free end of the painter is already looped around bumper, eye bolt, or other attachment on the vehicle.

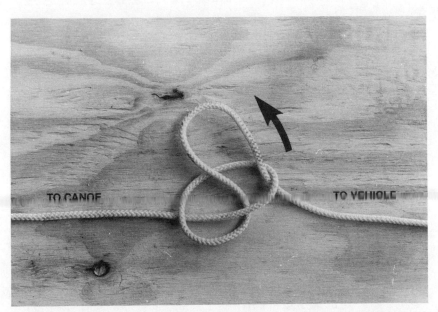

TO CANOE   TO VEHICLE

Bring slack up in an open loop and put this loop through the first one.

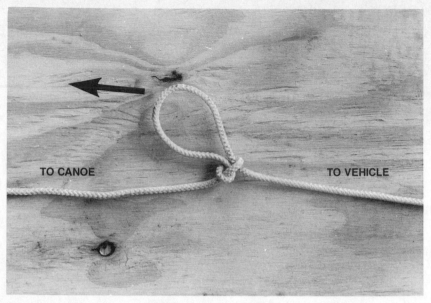

Pull the loops into a knot.

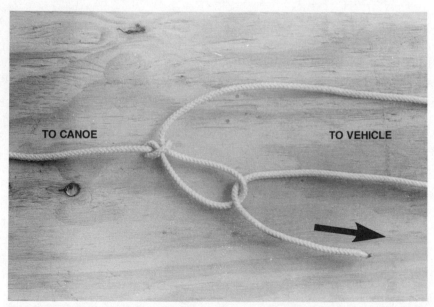

Run the very end of the free end through the loop. Pull in a downward direction until the painter is as tight as you want it.

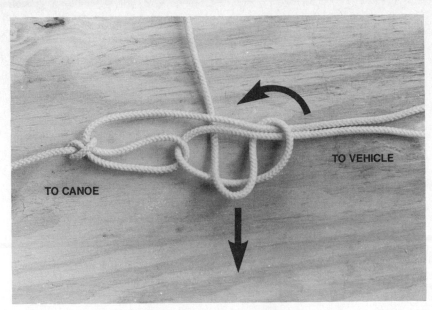

Hold the tension and loop back in.

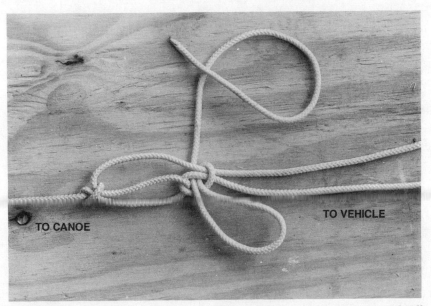

Still holding the tension, pull the loop tight. To untie, pull on the loose end. All loops will pull out, leaving your painter knot-free.

water to snag on something or loose in the hull to possibly catch your feet if you spill.

There are several patented devices available for pulling painters down tight. Most are good, but a rope tied in a trucker's hitch knot is just as good, and costs only the time it takes to learn to tie it. It holds fast, puts a lot of tension on the rope, loosens with a single pull, but stays tied unless it's deliberately loosened. Locate the hitches up in view of the driver, though, just in case you had an attention lapse when you tied them.

Canoe Carriers (Racks)

Canoe carriers, even the best of racks, should not be relied on to hold a canoe down to the car – the painters do that; the racks just provide a sturdy, safe platform on which the boats ride. Carriers fall into two big categories, bar racks and cushions. The bar type comes in one and two canoe widths (commonly about 60 and 78 inches).

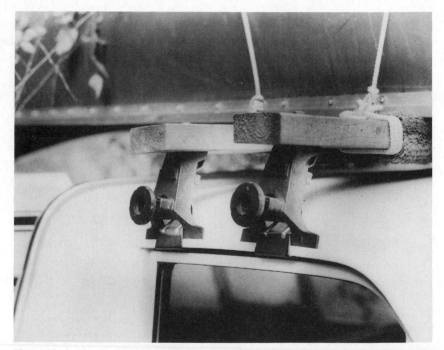

Homemade 2 x 4 wood racks on commercial clamps for vehicles with rain gutters. Note the carpeting on the cross bars.

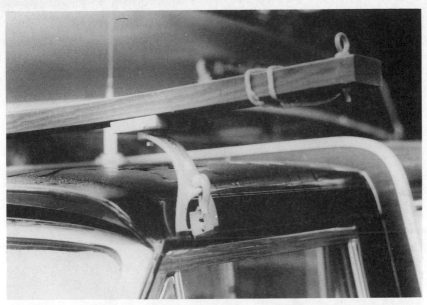

Another 2 x 4 cross bar with different clamps and with eye bolts for tying down the canoe.

Homemade square-metal-tubing racks on angle supports, bolted to a camper shell.

Although it's not too efficient, one-canoe racks *can* carry two canoes and a two-canoe rack can handle three boats.

Bar racks for cars with rain gutters have four brackets that clamp to the gutters. These are usually metal, and tighten down with a ratcheted wheel, a cam, or some similar device. A pair of brackets holds a cross bar, usually aluminum, some with a padded strip on the

Rack, support, and clamp for vehicles with no rain gutters. (Photo courtesy Yakima of California)

top. Cross tiedowns of nylon straps or rope come with some of them. The location of these straps in relation to the boat's gunwale may or may not be adjustable. The location of the brackets on the bar is adjustable to fit the car-top width. Some brackets can also be bought separately, and you can put your own metal or 2x4 wood cross bars on them. One specialty type of bracket is used for camper shells, and screws or bolts to the camper.

Carriers for cars without rain gutters commonly use some sort of hooks in the car door line and an adjustable-length connector between the bar and the car (often aircraft cable). The racks are supported by padded braces that rest on the car top.

Cushion foam or pad carriers are strictly one-boat carriers, useless for shuttling. The most common of this type consists of four foam blocks slotted to fit the canoe's gunwale. They sit directly on the car top. One version is double-slotted (top and bottom) to fit on station-wagon luggage carriers. The kits normally come with gutter and bumper hooks and tiedown ropes or straps. Some hook to the rain gutter and some to the car door line (for cars with no rain gutters).

Foam carriers that fit on the canoe's gunwales. These are usually supplied with all tiedowns and clamps.

Cross Tiedowns

Cross tiedowns secure the canoe to the racks or, in the case of pads, to the car. With pads they are usually nylon straps, rope, or elastic ropes that cross the hull and secure to the door line or the rain gutters with S hooks or brackets. Some have tightening devices such as buckles or D rings, others simply tie down.

Racks use the same basic devices except that the tiedowns attach to the racks. Rubber straps such as used for tarp tiedowns on trucks are frequently used on racks. These have an S hook in each end and are stretched over the hull. Many canoeists close up the inner hook so it stays on the racks and just hook the other end after it's over the boat. A rope and the trucker's hitch are also often used. Eye bolts are often used in wooden cross bars to attach the cross tiedowns to the rack. Commonly there is one on each end for a single canoe, and one in the middle and one on each outboard end for two canoes. Whether home-made or factory built, it's a good idea to position your tiedowns close to the gunwales of the boat as an extra aid in preventing side slip on the racks.

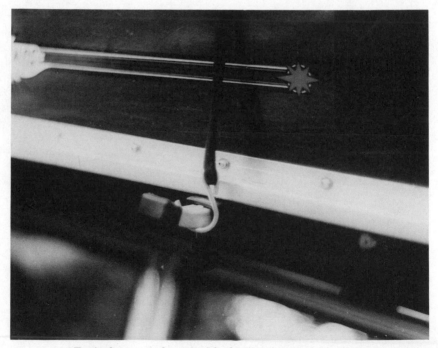

Typical cross tiedowns with elastic straps and S hooks.

Miscellaneous Items

Canteens/Water Bottles

Drinking water out of a running river may give *you* the runs – or worse. Canteens are the answer. Metal canteens are noisy; the plastic varieties are quieter and they do just as good a job of holding water – which, after all, is their primary purpose. Whatever you use, see that there is some way to attach it to the boat, then attach it with a cord or small rope. Don't leave enough slack in the cord or rope to entangle you. Coolness can be maintained longer by keeping the canteen out of the sun, by having a cover on it that you can wet periodically (evaporation cools the contents), or by freezing the full canteen the night before (without cap unless you want a burst or severely bloated canteen)!

First Aid Kit

Although it's not actually canoeing equipment, you should carry a first aid kit along on all trips. A small personal kit is a good beginning, but the kit should be larger and more comprehensive as the number of paddlers on a trip increases. Don't, however, get it so large and cumbersome you're tempted to leave it behind. Likely common maladies and ills on the river are cuts, burns from wind, sun, and fire, splinters, bruises, headaches, and insect stings. Possible misadventures could also include heatstroke, heat exhaustion, and snakebite. For winter canoeing, add frostbite and hypothermia to the list. Many of these can be satisfactorily taken care of with the minimal equipment that most basic first aid kits include (except for frostbite and hypothermia). A "space blanket" in the winter is a good idea. Add in other needed items such as tweezers, aspirin, and salt tablets. If you or anyone on the trip has some particular allergy, such as to insect bites, be sure to take along (or see that they do) the specific medicine required for it. If your first aid kit isn't in a waterproof container, be sure it's stored in something that *is* waterproof while on the trip.

Bailers

If you get large quantities of water in your canoe, it's most practical to just dump it out, but small amounts are more handily removed with a bailer. A bailer isn't anything fancy; as far as I know, they aren't even commercially available. Although they can be formed of fiberglass or wood or plastic and become quite exotic, a cheap and perfectly serviceable one can be made from any gallon or half-gallon

The inimitable bailer and sponge – simple, cheap, and always useful!

plastic jug with a built-in handle. Cut off the bottom part to suit your-self and leave the cap screwed on the top part. Tie one end of about two feet of ⅛-inch nylon rope to the bailer handle and tie the other end around a big sponge. Bailers and sponges are not tied in, just held in the boat ready for action by looping the rope over a thwart. The sponge is used like a mop after you remove most of the water with the bailer.

Waterproof Containers

All your river trip supplies will probably get soggy if you don't put them in something waterproof. This can be merely provoking if it's lunch, dead serious if it happens to be your extra clothes on a winter trip. Some items (cameras, binoculars, and the like) also require pro-tection from impact – at least if you ever intend to use them again!

Far and away the best all-around choice for a one-day trip is a government surplus ammunition box (also now available simply as a commercial storage box). They're metal and they're heavy, rigid, and noisy, but they're also waterproof, impact resistant, floatable, secure, and easy of access. They are available in four basic sizes, but the ones that are roughly 5½ inches wide, 11 inches long, and 7 inches deep seem most useful and popular. Check the box for pin holes (rust) and the seal on the lid for proper seating and continuity before you buy it, then test it in a tub of water overnight before you take it on the river. Painting it a light color will help keep its contents cooler and render it less likely to be forgotten. Ammo boxes are ideal for one-day trips or any trips when you're taking a camera or other optical goods. Pad the box with foam to prevent the fragiles from rattling around or let the other items you have in the box provide the padding (particularly if you like squashed sandwiches).

Many heavy-duty plastic bags are available. Made specifically for canoe use, they are various sized, waterproof, and very useful, especially for lightweight items without sharp corners. Some are double-walled (you blow up the outside bag for impact resistance and flotation), and some of these double-walled designs are specifically intended to protect optical goods. Nearly all the bags will hold some air (thus float), and some are tough enough to be used as inflated seats on shore. Some flotation bags open at the end so they can also be used as waterproof storage. These are of particular interest to the solo paddler.

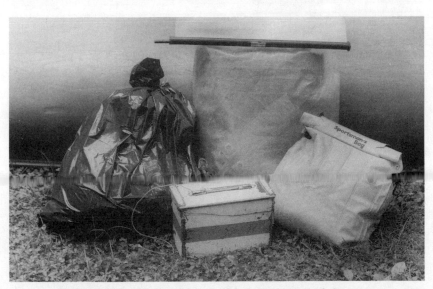

Various watertight containers with several types of closures.

Plastic pickle or relish (or whatever) buckets in the two-, three-, or five-gallon sizes work well too, unless you select one whose plastic becomes brittle and breakable in cold weather. Two garbage bags, each tied and placed one inside the other, will do for soft items without sharp corners or edges; the bags are rather fragile, however.

These are just a few ways to protect your goods. Whatever waterproofing container you use, however, tie it or wedge it in so it's secure.

A typical summer outfit.

Clothing

Dress for the season, the weather, and the water temperature, and always with the anticipation of getting wet. In the summer and on warm water, this can mean shorts and a shirt or almost anything that suits you and doesn't get you arrested. In the winter, or on cold waters in the summer, it can mean anything up to and including wet suits. Do remember that clothes are protection not only from cold, wind, and sun but also from abrasion. River rocks are often sharp, and so are the rough edges of some canoes.

Hats and Caps

In the summer, a cap or hat is good sun protection, cuts down on eye strain, and is a godsend for paddlers who wear glasses and are out in the rain. In cold weather, head covering is vital to prevent the tremendous heat loss your body suffers if this extremity is left uncovered.

Raingear

Use a rain suit. Ponchos and raincoats flap, flop, catch on things, interfere with your paddling, and could be dangerous if you spill and they snag on something. Besides this, they are poor rain protection for an active paddler. Use a rain suit with close-fitting waist, ankles, and cuffs. All rain suits trap condensation from the moisture and heat of your body, but the newer materials such as Gore-Tex do a better job of preventing this condition (at a considerably higher cost) than the old standbys of coated nylon and the like. Most rain suits also have some vents built in to help with condensation, but they're not much help. If you have on a wet suit, you obviously do not need rain protection.

Paddling jackets and pants are good. These are waterproof, fit snugly around waist, neck, wrists, and ankles, and help keep you dry from splash and rain, but they don't do much for sweat and condensation. They're great on low-temperature rivers in the summer when you get splashed and as a final, windproof covering over anything.

Shoes

Always wear shoes to protect your feet from rocks, sticks, and the broken glass, open cans, and other debris that thoughtless idiots toss on riverbanks and bottoms. Holey river shoes are usually sneakers with naturally worn-out drain holes in them. These often trap a lot of

Paddling pants and jackets protect you from rain and splash and add warmth on cold rivers.

grit, sand, and gravel. "Jellies" are plastic, open-weave strap-on shoes resembling sandals that are atrocious looking (I think), but they do not trap half the river bottom. Wet-suit booties are usually worn in cold weather/cold water canoeing, commonly with a jelly or some oversize sneaker over them to protect the Neoprene, unless the booties have built-in soles.

Except for the booties, slip-on shoes are likely to slip *off* in current. Use the tie-on type.

Cold-Weather Clothing

Cold-weather canoeing requires more concern in dressing. You want warmth and dryness, but you also want warmth if you get wet and you do not want to drown because of a mass of soggy, heavy clothing. Dressing in three layers is a good way to solve all these problems if you're not out in wet-suit weather. The outer layer provides wind and splash protection, the middle layer gives warmth, and the inner layer either wicks moisture away from your body (if you're not soaked) or conserves warmth if you are.

Windbreakers, paddling pants and jackets, or rain suits give good outer-layer protection. All are usually of some coated material such as nylon or one of the breathable fabrics such as Gore-Tex. Most are snug fitting at the cuffs, ankles, waist, and neck.

Wool or one of the synthetics such as pile or Thinsulate make a good "warmth" layer. Wool is still the best natural fiber insulation, although pile or bunting runs it a close second. Pile is a fluffy polyester that gives almost the same warmth as wool but at less weight. Both wool and pile retain much of their warmth when wet – you just need to wring out the excess moisture. Thinsulate (and its competitors) have combination materials. They work by reflecting radiant heat from the body back to the body. Such garments are usually backed by some form of pile insulation. Down loses all its insulating value when wet. It also becomes very heavy, thus dangerous. Cotton has little insulating value to begin with and actually wicks water into itself. Some of the synthetics, though warm, are too bulky and movement-restricting for their warmth and very weighty if they get wet.

Wool makes a good inner layer too, for the same reasons it is a good warmth layer. Polypropylene underwear is also good. This is often combined with wool or pile lining for warmth and has the advantage of wicking body moisture away from your body. Silk underwear is soft, comfortable, and also wicks moisture away. Obviously all this underwear should be full length, long-john style, and of a weight commensurate with the conditions expected.

Head, hand, and foot covering is very important. The body loses a tremendous amount of heat through uncovered or poorly insulated extremities. Caps, hoods, gloves or mittens, wool socks, and wet-suit booties will do a good job of keeping this heat loss down. You might also investigate one of the various styles of mittens that let you grip the paddle with your bare skin yet cover your hands.

Wet Suits

Wet suits are not just conveniences, adding a definite degree of comfort to a cold-water or cold-weather trip; they can also be life savers. Nothing else does as much toward keeping you warm on a raw, windy, wet, low-temperature day. Wet suits keep you warm by holding a very thin layer of river water between your body and the Neoprene of the suit. Your body warms this layer, the Neoprene of the suit

Ridiculous looking, but effective: "Pogies" allow bare hands on the paddle, but protect them from the elements.

insulates and holds the warmth. In a good-fitting suit, the inevitable flow and exchange of this layer of water as you move is slow enough so your body always keeps the fresh water warm.

Wet suits are made of Neoprene, a rubber compound that has had nitrogen bubbled through it to form thousands of tiny little air pockets. Of the two methods of nitrogen bubbling, gas-blown is the best, but the other method – chemically blown – is cheaper.

Neoprene thickness affects insulation value, but too-thick material also restricts movement. Generally $\frac{1}{8}$ or $\frac{3}{16}$-inch material is good for general canoe usage. Wet suits need to be close-fitting for best warmth but not too tight. Suits designed for canoeing are usually the best, because they're cut to provide more room in the arms, shoulders, and

Three styles of wet suits: short "Farmer John" with sleeveless jacket; full two-piece suit with "beaver tail"; and a female tailored sleeveless one-piece.

behind the knees. Some also offer extra padding in the knee area. There are also men's and women's cuts that allow for the physical differences of the gender, or you can buy custom-built suits that fit exactly.

Wet suits when they get wet are hard to get on and off, so some are lined with nylon to make this task easier. Nylon outer linings are also available to help protect the material, but many paddlers accomplish the same result by wearing clothes or a jumpsuit over the wet suit. Another help in wet-suit donning is zippers. These are of some corrosion-resisting material. Depending upon the style of the suit, the zippers may be in the legs, arms, or chest, or various combinations of these. Some suits are slip-on and have no zippers.

Wet suits come in various styles—one piece with full or thigh-length legs and no arms, zippered jackets with long arms, pullover jackets with no arms, two-piece full suits, almost any style you may want. One jacket style has a Neoprene body and loose-fitting, coated nylon sleeves, the idea being to combine torso warmth with maximum arm movement. Many paddlers prefer a short "Farmer John" type suit and add a jacket in very cold weather. As a matter of interest, wet suits are usually worn over a bathing suit or undergarments only.

The question of when to wear a wet suit depends on when you think you may need it. We all feel the cold differently. One good rule of thumb, however, is to put it on any time the combined air and water temperature doesn't add up to 100 degrees.

Wet-suit booties, gloves or mittens, and head coverings complete the Neoprene outfits. These are all well worth the investment, as the body loses a tremendous amount of heat through uncovered extremities, particularly in the low temperatures of wet-suit weather.

It's strange how styles and ideas seem to forever recycle. Although wet suits are still the favorite cold-weather dress, their predecessors—dry suits—are now regaining favor in the low-temperature canoeing market. In a well-fitted dry suit you stay dry; the suit material shields you from the cold water, and your clothing provides the insulation to retain your body warmth. Hand and foot covering is your choice; you can have wet or dry.

Random Reminders

Tying In

If you intend to take it with you, then tie or attach it to the canoe some way so it really will go with you and won't be washed out if you spill or swamp. An extra paddle in a solo canoe can usually be jammed in between your flotation and the hull, seats, or thwarts of the canoe. Some paddlers tuck the blade (only) under the lacing of one air bag and tie the grip end to a thwart with a bow knot. Take a little care with this, however; the necessity for the spare paddle usually occurs when

One way to carry a spare paddle so it's secure but handy.

you have no time to fight one loose from a wedged-in, awkward position. One end wedged and one end tied is usually a better way. If you have room tie the extra paddle in under a thwart or seat (it won't float away so easily if you swamp), blade on the hull, grip facing you and in a handy position to grab if you need it. Tie the grip end with a bow knot. Use string that can be easily broken by hitting the grip downward with your hand in case the knot jams.

Tie your lunch, extra clothes, and so on with light rope and hard knots or wedge them in between the canoe and your flotation; preferably do both. You won't be needing them frequently. Use cord and a bow knot for your canteen. Loop your bailer and sponge string over a handy reachable thwart; you don't need to tie it. Attach everything out of your way so it doesn't slither along the hull and interfere with your paddling or entangle your feet.

Of particular importance to those who wear glasses is to remember to tie them on your head. Use string around or through drilled holes in the earpieces, or get one of the adjustable elastic bands sold for sports use. Folks with contacts just have to remember to close their eyes before they hit the water.

Remember that loose ropes and strings in the bottom of a canoe can be dangerous if they whip around your arm, leg, or body when you spill. Painters are the worst; keep them tied up short or tucked in behind your flotation or elsewhere out of the way. Make sure any other ropes, straps, strings, or cords holding equipment in are long enough to do their job but not do a job on you!

Car Keys, Wallets, and Pocket Items

Get everything out of your pockets that can be ruined by water or could be troublesome if you lost it. This includes such things as wallets, keys, cigarettes, and snacks (which *do* melt). Put them all in something waterproof; it's a good idea to assume you *are* going in the water!

Mark It

There's a lot of identical equipment out on the rivers, so identify all your equipment with your name, address, and telephone number, including area code. Use a waterproof felt pen in a contrasting color on paddles, ammo boxes, and other firm surfaces. Paint the information on knee pads, and use cloth or tape labels stuck or sewed on for other items.

A Word About Ice Chests

Ice chests have little place in a solo canoe. They're bulky, heavy, make the boat harder to rescue if that's required, and there's usually no room for them anyway! I have seen paddlers fit a small chest into a hollowed-out place in their foam flotation and others wedge them between hull and air bags, but I still don't like carrying them. However, I'm always willing to share whatever is in one that *is* brought along!

4

Some Paddle Stroke Basics

There are some basic things you need to know about paddling. Basic and maybe boring, but important and necessary – unless you plan to just beat the water to death and wear yourself out in the process. If you go through this short little chapter carefully (and don't doze off), you'll better understand the reasons for some of the things in the next two chapters.

Paddle Grip

You waste a lot of effort holding your paddle incorrectly. The grip of the paddle is to be held in your hand; don't hold the paddle shaft *below* the grip. Just as important is the distance between your hands on the paddle. Too small a distance gives you little leverage, poor control, and an insecure grip; too great a distance reduces both reach and paddle control.

While you are learning to paddle, a good rule of thumb is to have the distance between your hands six to twelve inches greater than your shoulder width. Another guide is to hold the paddle over your

A paddle grip that is too short. This drastically reduces power and control.

A paddle grip that is too long. It's not only awkward, but reduces reach.

The "right-angle arms" method of finding a good beginning hand spread on a paddle.

head with both forearms at a 90-degree angle. Either way will give you a good starting position. Once you've achieved some paddling efficiency, you'll automatically assume the correct grip and also be changing it slightly in various situations.

Power Faces

The power face of a paddle blade is the side that presses against the water in a normal forward stroke. This is no particular blade side, only a reference in any given stroke. Continuous power on the blade can be maintained if the same power face is used throughout any given stroke. Changing power faces (flipping the paddle around in your hand so that the other side of the blade is pushing against the water) during a stroke is generally less efficient. Turning the blade does nothing to help you and, in some cases, works against you. That's the reason you'll find such emphasis on the orientation of the hands in this book: careful attention to this hand orientation will automatically put the blade in position to keep the same power face, whether you're doing a "pure" stroke or a combination of strokes. This hand orientation is usually described in terms of upper-hand thumb position, such as thumb down (toward the water) or thumb up (toward the sky). *But*—to weasel—there *are* some strokes in which you *will* find the power face deliberately reversed!

Paddle Force

Paddle force is what makes your canoe move where you want it to. As the flat of the paddle blade is what transmits this force from you to the water and then to the hull, the relation of this flat to where you want to direct the force is very important. Efficient paddle strokes depend greatly on being sure of the direction of force and on directing this force where you want it. This can be done only by careful attention to blade angle and, in some strokes, to the point in the stroke when the power is applied.

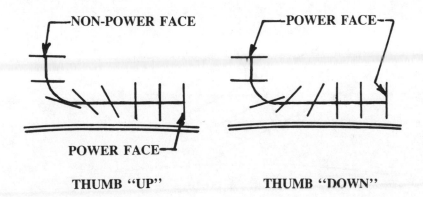

NON-POWER FACE   POWER FACE

POWER FACE

THUMB "UP"   THUMB "DOWN"

In the drawing the dotted lines represent the force of a paddle pushing against the water. This major force will always be perpendicular to the flat of the blade. The heavy solid line shows the direction you want the canoe to move when you do this stroke, and the other solid lines show the direction that the force of the blade is actually pushing the canoe.

In the next drawing the lines represent the same things, but the blade is out of line with the desired direction. Angling the blade like this causes the force to push the canoe in a different direction from the one you want. This means your stroke is inefficient (extra work) and you must put some correction on it to make the boat go where you want (more extra work). All in all, you're wasting a lot of energy. Always have the blade face square with the direction you want the boat to move. This does not necessarily mean in line with some part of the boat, as you may well want to move the boat diagonally.

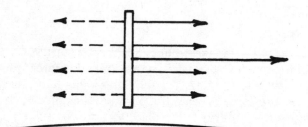

SIDE OF HULL

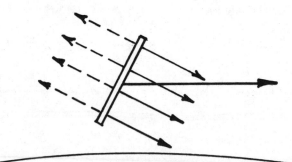

SIDE OF HULL

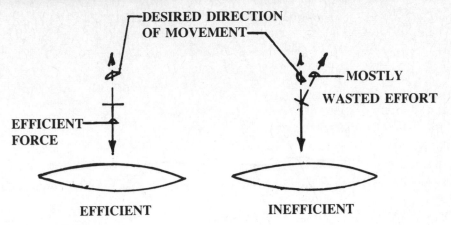

EFFICIENT INEFFICIENT

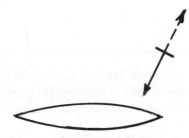

DIAGONAL DRAW

FINE, BECAUSE YOU WANT TO GO DIAGONALLY

The same principle applies to the vertical part of your paddle strokes. In the illustration you're looking at a typical forward paddle stroke as viewed from the side of the canoe. You'll see that at the start of the stroke some of the force is aimed downward, which serves to push up the side of the canoe on your paddle side. At the end of the stroke some force is directed upward; you're "lifting" water and pulling down on that side of the canoe. In the middle you're ideal; all your force is directed in a 180-degree direction from your desired movement.

Most paddle strokes, then, are broken into three segments: the entry where the power face is angled down, the power part in the middle, and the end of the stroke where the blade is angled up. Both

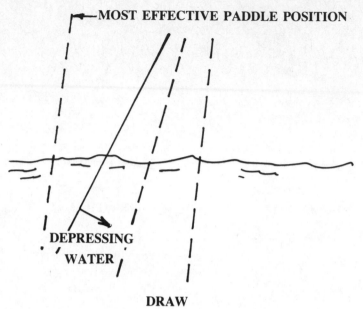

DRAW

the start and end positions in strokes such as the back and forward stroke should be more relaxed, with the real power being applied in the middle, the short distance just before, through, and just after the perpendicular blade position.

Obviously, you can't keep a paddle in the middle position all through a stroke without some awkward rocking body movements. Do try, however, to avoid wasting a lot of your effort in up or down components. To avoid this, don't reach too far forward (unless accompanied by a body lean forward) and cut off the power of your stroke before it's doing more harm than good. Your goal is to move the canoe, not pick up or depress the river.

Vertical Paddles

In addition to keeping the power face of your blade perpendicular to the direction of the "push" you want, you also need to keep the whole paddle perpendicular to the surface of the water unless you are intentionally off vertical (as when doing sweeps). Keeping the paddle vertical allows more of the blade to be in the water during more of the stroke, reduces the turning force of an inclined paddle, and, as we have already seen, directs the paddle force more accurately.

Arm and Hand Position

The only power in a solo canoe is you, and you're located near the center of the hull. In this position the turning effect of a paddle stroke on the canoe is much less than it would be if you were near one end of the hull. This is an advantage if you want to go in a straight line or make sweeping turns, a disadvantage if you want to pivot or make a sharper turn. To offset this disadvantage, you have to apply the principles of leverage to your paddle strokes, which, in solo usage, means that you have to reach farther—forward, backward, or to the side as the case may be. Generally, the farther the blade extends toward bow or stern the greater the turning moment will be.

This does not mean you should reach to the point of awkwardness, unbalancing the boat or falling out of it, and obviously this generality

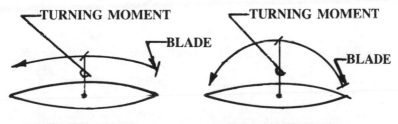

LESS EFFICIENT   MORE EFFICIENT

A SWEEP

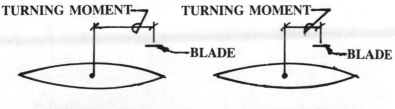

MORE EFFICIENT   LESS EFFICIENT

A BRACE

does not apply to all paddle strokes or techniques. You will use all kinds of variations and combinations, depending on what you are trying to do. But realize that a force acting farther away from your body will do things to the hull faster and easier than that same force applied closer to your body.

The key is a combination of lean (body and boat) and position of hand, arm, and paddle. You can get a greater reach by leaning forward, backward, or to the paddle side; twisting the body at the waist; simply straightening out the arms; and often just by moving the arms

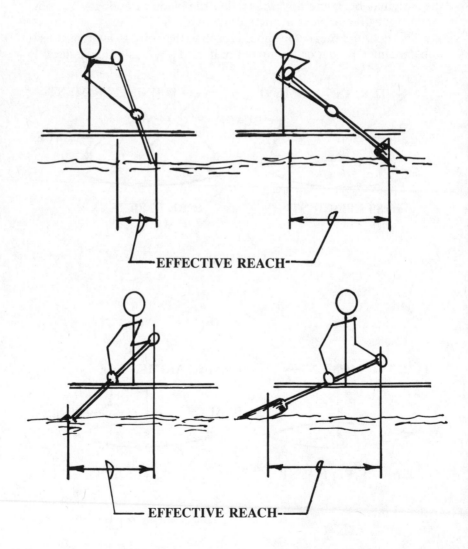

EFFECTIVE REACH

EFFECTIVE REACH

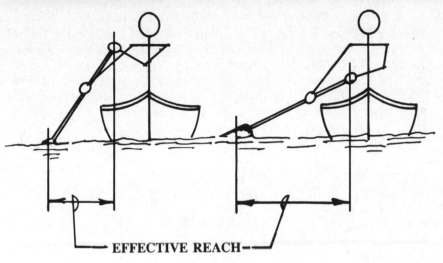

EFFECTIVE REACH

in a certain way.

One good example of this is a high brace done toward the bow. In one drawing the paddler has his upper hand over his shoulder and on his "off" paddle side. In the other sketch nothing has changed except that the paddler has brought his upper hand over to his paddle side and lowered the grip.

Here's another example, a simple stern pry or the correction part of a hook J or forward-correction stroke. All the paddler has done to increase the reach or leverage of the stroke is to bring his upper hand down closer to the gunwale. Viewed from the front, the same lowering of one hand increases the effectiveness of a sweep. The point of all of this is simple: small factors can make a big difference in paddling efficiency, leverage, and force.

Your Position in the Canoe

The standard way to stay as stable, as in control, and as least likely to fall out of a solo canoe as possible is the three-point kneeling position. Your center of gravity is low and you're braced at three points: your knees in the bilges and your buttocks against a thwart, the edge of a seat, your flotation, or on the saddle. Most of your weight is on your knees unless you're on a saddle. This position allows you to use your leg and body muscles, something you can't do very well when sitting on the seat.

If you have a well-fitted solo saddle, your position will vary depending on what kind of saddle you have, but sitting in it should be very stable, even more so than the traditional three-point stance. There is still actually a basic three-point contact, but it's enhanced because you can brace your legs against the side or front of the saddle while the saddle holds you more in position fore and aft. Regardless of your support method, it's important to not be too low in the hull. A common error is for paddlers to slide down and actually sit on the

The "three-point" kneeling posture against a thwart — knees spread and buttocks resting against thwart.

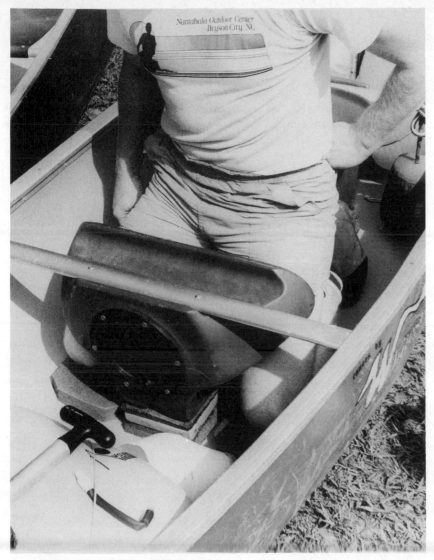

Saddles give a three-point kneeling position plus the security of leg grip.

backs of their calves; this position reduces reach, cuts down on control and paddler stability, and contributes to legs going to sleep. A posture with the buttocks resting level with or a little below the gunwale will normally be satisfactory, comfortable, and efficient. This, however, is something you have to work out yourself.

Important: In an actual solo canoe, one designed for solo usage, you will normally kneel or sit centered in the boat's width. This is partly for balance, partly for advantageous paddling on both sides, and partly because these "hot" little boats have a tendency to turn in the direction of the weight shift. Technically, this centered position applies to any canoe paddled solo, but in a larger, standard cruising hull, you will probably find it more practical to sit slightly to the side of the canoe in which you normally paddle, at least out on the smoother portions of the rivers where rapid maneuvering isn't required.

Use of the Body, Legs, and Stomach

Your torso and leg muscles are generally much stronger than your arm and shoulder muscles. As I mentioned before, the three-point kneeling position allows you to bring these powerful muscles into play in the canoe. Thigh straps, foot blocks, and saddles help you use them even more. One of your goals in solo canoeing should be to make your canoe an extension of your body so that when you move, it moves.

An overenthusiastic lean in action!

While this isn't too important in straight-ahead or back paddling, it is important in making turns. It means using the body to assist the boat's movements. The stomach and thighs are particularly helpful. In any turning movement, try to actually twist the boat into the turn with your legs and stomach muscles instead of relying on the paddle alone. Obviously this is easier in a lightweight little slalom boat than in a full-size recreational canoe.

Leaning a solo canoe also helps it turn. When the boat is heeled over toward the direction of the turn, there is usually less hull in the water and thus less resistance. This is done by leaning the body to the inside of the turn while using hip and knee pressure to heel the boat even farther over. (Your body stays more or less perpendicular to the plane of the river). The simultaneous combination of leaning, twisting the boat with the legs, and putting power on the paddle stroke gives much faster, more effective turns. This is particularly true if you're paddling a little hotshot pure solo boat. You'll pay for this at first with sore thigh and stomach muscles, but keep at it—it will make your maneuvers much more effective.

Swapping Sides

Random swapping of paddle sides in a tandem canoe invokes the more or less polite ridicule of experienced canoeists, the fury of serious canoeing instructors, and unkind remarks from the partner who just got dumped because both of you were suddenly paddling on the same side. Not so in the world of solo canoeing; here swapping sides is

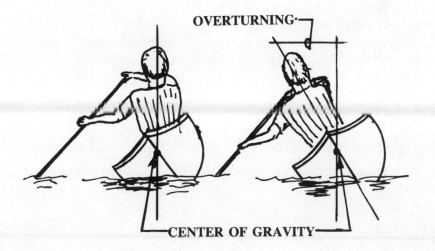

done often and is considered not only socially acceptable but also (on occasion) the wisest course to follow. This does not mean swapping because you never learned how to do something otherwise. It means swapping because either you're tired of paddling on the same side or there's a definite reason for swapping. As you go through this book you'll find some of those reasons.

5

Paddle Techniques

In this and the next chapter you'll learn how to do the various basic solo paddle strokes. Out on the river (once you've mastered these "pure" methods of doing the strokes), you'll blend and combine and probably alter these strokes at the behest of circumstance and your own experience. The major thing now, however, is to learn how to do the basic strokes in a generally accepted correct and efficient way.

One thing that will help you a lot is to understand what each stroke is intended to do and the basic concept of how it does it. It's simple cause and effect, but I have learned through many years of teaching river canoeing that students often put the cart before the horse; they grasp this important relationship of cause and effect *after* learning the details. So get the big idea first, then work on the technicalities. Some of the strokes are very simple; others require more thinking to do correctly. All require practice and attention to the details that make them easier to do, correct, and efficient. Obviously you can't learn everything from this book (or any other book), so don't expect to. You'll have to do some thinking on your own, watch other paddlers, ask questions, try various things, and, above all, paddle and practice!

Some Rules and Definitions

There are a few rules about solo paddling that should be strictly observed until they become automatic. They'll help you get more out of your paddle strokes and be a more efficient paddler, too.

Rule: Use all of your blade that's needed. A paddle blade does no good waving around in the air and only half as much good as it should if only half the blade needed is submerged. In general most of the blade should be in the water. There are exceptions, such as sweeps, where the blade is only partially submerged. On the other hand don't "drown" your paddle. Burying it too deep isn't necessary and, in some cases, destroys the efficiency of the stroke. Submerge the blade as much as necessary but don't go any deeper with it.

Rule: Do complete strokes. Partial strokes give partial results. If a stroke is to be most effective, you need to give it its full swing, not stop partway through.

Rule: Learn the various strokes; they all have their uses. A river is rarely one long mass of rapids with no pools or flat places. Therefore, you need to learn how to negotiate the pools and other "cruising" areas as well as those full of obstructions. Then too, you won't always be running rapids. You may do more cruising than you think down rivers where holding a course or fighting wind effect is more important than making sudden maneuvers.

Rule: Use the right stroke at the right time. There are many different paddle strokes. Some are best used when you have a lot of time and distance in which to do something; others are most useful when quick direction changes are necessary.

Rule: Learn the pure strokes first and learn them well before you begin varying them. Paddle techniques are the foundation of successful solo

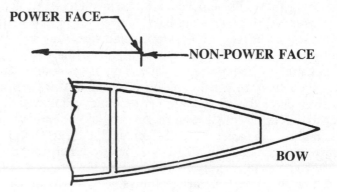

maneuvering, and successful maneuvering is the key to keeping your canoe (and maybe you) in one piece. Learning the correct way to do a pure stroke gives you a solid base on which to build. Slopping through paddle strokes wastes energy, time, and now and then a canoe.

Rule: Pure strokes are rarely used. Uh-oh! Then why learn them? Because you will use pure strokes at first but, as your paddling experience broadens, you'll begin to incorporate more and more little adjustments into the strokes to compensate for wind and wave and course corrections. You'll also begin to do more and more blending of strokes. Still, pure strokes give you a solid foundation upon which to incorporate these variations.

Definition: Power face. The power face of your blade is whichever flat side of the blade is being used to exert force on the water in any particular stroke or sequence of strokes. Either blade face may be used as the initial power face. In this chapter and the next one, and to ensure that your wrist and arm motions and paddle orientation are right as you work on a particular stroke, the power face for any given stroke is always assumed to be the side of your blade that is facing and being moved toward the stern when you have the paddle in position for a basic forward stroke. The other side of your blade will be called the non-power face.

Definition: Feathering. This is a paddle position used on the recovery part of many strokes. In this position the edge of the blade slices

A feathered recovery, the paddle-blade edge on to wind and wave.

through waves and wind on above-water recoveries and through the water on underwater recoveries. This cuts down on the work you have to do and, in the case of waves, reduces the chances of the canoe being jerked off course or the paddle being pulled from your hand.

Finally, there are usually a few key points in doing any paddle stroke that, if observed, make the whole stroke easier to do efficiently. I've tried to describe the strokes thoroughly enough so you don't make an error in some of these often small but vital things. Look at the photos and drawings as you go through the descriptions and try to visualize what the stroke is doing to the canoe as well as what you are supposed to be doing with the paddle. Common sense will often help you if you get confused. Pay particular attention to your hand positions; if they are right, that will automatically put your paddle blade in the correct position. As silly as it may sound, a good way to dry-practice the strokes is to kneel on a sofa, bed, coffee table, or something similar and, paddle in hand, go through the motions step by step.

Going Forward

There are four basic ways of propelling the solo canoe forward and steering it at the same time: the forward stroke, the forward sweep (or one of its variations), the C stroke, and the forward correction (hook J) stroke. The last two are variations of the basic forward stroke. All these move the boat forward and all "steer" the canoe, simply because they all turn the boat one way or another, but the last two are usually considered the actual steering strokes. Sweeps are so important that I've treated them separately. One other technique, the stationary draw, also steers the canoe but applies no power.

The Forward Stroke

Except for the very beginning and recovery parts of this stroke, hold the paddle so both hands are out over the water and the paddle is vertical to the water. Do not lay the paddle over at an angle with the grip inboard. You'll find this vertical position rather awkward at first, but work at it until it's automatic. It's the most efficient position and will give you less trouble in steering the canoe.

The face of the paddle is perpendicular to the keel and the stroke is done *parallel* to the keel line, not following the curved edge of the gunwale. This is important, as it allows you to get the fullest useful power from the stroke. Another important point is to use both arms for

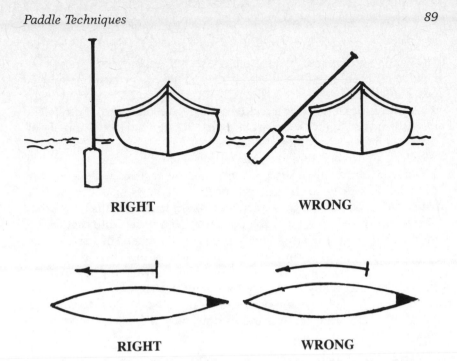

the power. Don't hold with one hand and pull or push with the other; simultaneously push with the upper hand and pull with the lower. This uses the principles of the lever in multiplying the force of your stroke, but doesn't rely on only one arm to do most of the work.

An Important Point (Cause and Effect)

The forward stroke always turns the boat *away* from your paddle side, regardless of which side you are paddling on.

STROKE

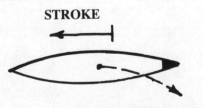

BOAT TURNS AWAY FROM PADDLE

Details

Bend your upper arm at the elbow so your upper hand is near your head and six inches or so in front of it. This upper hand should be outboard of your head, approximately above or just beyond the on-side gunwale of the canoe so the paddle is nearly vertical in the water. The lower arm is straight or almost straight. Rotate your body and shoulders so the lower arm shoulder is leading.

Push with your upper arm by straightening it, pushing forward and down. Simultaneously, pull with the lower arm, which remains extended or nearly so throughout most of the stroke. As you do this, rotate your body so the upper arm and shoulder lead. This unwinding of the torso provides a lot of the power in the stroke. Note that during the power part of the stroke both hands are outboard of the gunwale and the lower hand *always* remains in that position. The lower hand should, in general, also remain above the gunwale throughout the stroke. This isn't really necessary for the forward stroke, but it's a good habit to get into as it is important for some other paddle techniques.

Don't forget that for maximum efficiency the power face of the

The start of a forward stroke. The lower-arm shoulder is rotated forward.

The start of a forward stroke. Note the vertical position of the paddle in the water.

blade should stay as square to the path of the desired force as possible, so work to keep the blade as close to vertical as you can. Relax somewhat on the beginning of the stroke, put the power into it when the blade is near vertical (actually a rather short power part), then relax at the end of the stroke. Cut the power part of the stroke off about even with your hip. Both arms should now be fully extended or almost so and both hands out over the water.

Recovery

Recovery is above water. After stopping the power, relax and let your arms continue on in the natural swing of the stroke so the upper hand ends up about gunwale height above the water. The paddle blade will come to the surface naturally as you do this. *Do not lift* the paddle to recover it. (You may have to lift a little but this depends on your height and arm and paddle length.) Push down with the upper hand to raise the blade clear of the water a few inches, and swing the lower arm out and around in an arc toward the bow of the canoe so the paddle is more or less horizontal to the water (feathered) and the power face of the blade is up. The knuckles of both hands will be turned down toward the water, and the lower arm will be bent slightly. Keep the blade in this feathered position as you recover, and keep your arms relaxed. Keep your lower arm more or less straight. As your upper arm comes in across the gunwale, begin bringing the grip of the paddle diagonally upward toward your head into position for starting another stroke. As you do this, rotate your upper hand thumb up and

The end of a forward stroke. The arms are nearly straight, the body rotated so the upper-arm shoulder is forward.

in toward your face; this will turn the paddle blade so the power face will be in the correct position.

The Forward Correction Stroke (Hook J)

There are a number of traditional steering strokes for a canoe, the pitch J being one of the most hallowed. There are also a number of variations of this J; one adds a pry at the end of the stroke as a steering correction, and another is called the hook J. The basic difference between the last two is whether you turn your upper-hand thumb up or down and whether or not you pry off the side of the canoe. The forward correction stroke described here is really a crossbreed, but comes closest to the hook J. It's ungraceful and noisy, but very strong and efficient because it uses the principles of leverage to increase your paddle force and maintains the same power face throughout the stroke. I consider this version a much better solo river stroke than the J, and so will not go into any detail on the J itself. If you wish to learn the J, any good lake canoeing book will give you the fundamentals of it.

In the forward correction stroke, all the basic instructions on paddle position in the forward stroke apply, as the forward correction stroke is nothing but a simple, basic forward stroke with a stern pry on the end of it.

An Important Point (Cause and Effect)

The forward correction stroke first pushes the canoe *away* from the paddle side (during the "forward" part), then swings it back *to* the paddle side during the "correction" part. By varying the amount of forward and the amount of correction within a stroke, you can make the boat go straight, turn to your paddle side, or turn away from your paddle side a controlled amount.

Details

From the beginning of the stroke back to about even with your knee, all movements are done exactly as in the forward stroke except that rather than maintaining your stroke parallel to the keel, you let it gradually move in toward the gunwale. In other words, you violate one of the rules and somewhat follow the curve of the gunwale; you want to end up with the shaft of the paddle touching the gunwale.

When the paddle shaft reaches about your knee, start rotating your upper-hand thumb away from your face and down toward the water. As you rotate your upper hand, simultaneously turn the lower hand so the lower-hand knuckles also rotate outboard and down toward the water. This is the beginning of the correction or "hook" part of the stroke. The paddle blade should be completely turned up on its edge about the time your lower hand reaches a point in line with your hip. The paddle shaft should come in contact with the gunwale at the same moment. The upper arm should now be fully or almost fully extended and the upper hand about a foot above the gunwale and *directly over the gunwale*, not inboard. This puts the blade back behind you, up on its edge and close to the hull. The lower shaft of the paddle is actually touching the gunwale, and your lower hand should be just above the gunwale but not touching the canoe. The paddle will be angled forward, blade behind your hips, and grip toward the bow. All or nearly all of the blade will be below the surface of the water.

Note: Rotating the paddle "thumbs down" is the most efficient way of doing this stroke, because you do not change power faces. Many people, however, find this a difficult position. If you insist on doing it

The edge-up position of the blade on the "correction" of a forward-correction stroke. Note the upper hand rotation to a thumb-down position.

inefficiently, feel free to rotate your hands "thumbs up" and inboard and change power faces in the middle of the stroke.

The correction part of the stroke is applied by simply pulling straight *across* the boat with your upper hand, using the gunwale as a fulcrum and prying off of it. The lower hand does no work, only steadies the paddle and keeps it in contact with the gunwale. Stop pulling at about a 45-degree angle to the keel, or when the paddle grip reaches about the centerline of the canoe. More than this and you're going into a reverse sweep—which will certainly turn the canoe, but slows it down in the process. Do all of this stroke—forward and correction parts—in one smooth, continuous motion; don't make two separate movements of it.

For maximum efficiency the blade should really be on its edge, not

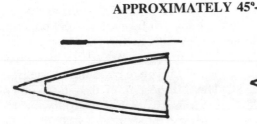

APPROXIMATELY 45°

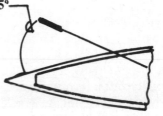

START POSITION   **END POSITION**

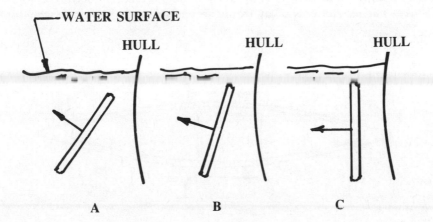

WATER SURFACE

HULL   HULL   HULL

A   B   C

sloped over at an angle one way or the other. A common error is failing to turn it enough. This results in part of the correcting force (which has to be to the side to do the most good) to instead be directed upward — lifting the river, pulling down the boat, and wasting all that good energy. Remember, keep the lower hand slightly above the gunwale, not resting on it. Develop wrist control; don't clamp the paddle to the gunwale with your fingers.

Recovery

Recovery is above water. Relax your arms, let the paddle float out of the water on its edge (or push the paddle grip down toward the hull a little), and recover over the surface with the paddle feathered in the same manner as for the forward stroke.

The C Stroke

The C stroke is identical to the hook J or forward correction stroke except for having an added correction part at the very beginning. It gets its name from the shape it traces in the water when viewed from above. Actually, it forms a C shape only if you're paddling on the right; on the left it forms a reversed C. The C is most often used in moving off from a dead start in a solo boat, although it's handy in a wind too. You'll probably use the other steering strokes more frequently once you're underway.

An Important Point (Cause and Effect)

The C stroke first pulls the bow *to* the paddle, the forward component pushes the bow *away* from the paddle, and the final correction

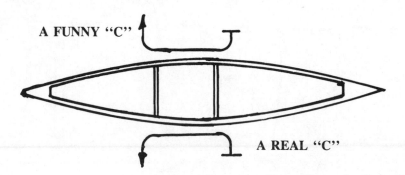

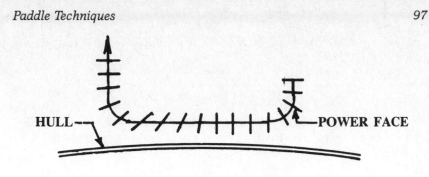

HULL POWER FACE

THE "C" STROKE

pulls the bow back again. As in the forward correction stroke, the idea is to balance the amount of each component to make the boat go where you want it – straight, right or left, without yawing all over the river.

Details

To begin the C stroke, reach forward as you would for a forward stroke, except turn the blade up on its edge, power face in toward the hull. Place the blade in the water 12 to 18 inches out from the hull (or whatever is comfortable for your reach). Your upper hand will be thumbs down with the palm of the hand facing forward toward the blade. Pull straight in toward the hull (do not put any forward component into this part) and, as you pull, gradually and smoothly turn the blade into the forward stroke position. Pull on back as in a forward stroke, begin your correction turn as required, and end up with your correctional pry (or J if you're using it) as necessary, just like in the forward correction stroke.

Recovery

The recovery is above the water as in the forward stroke.

The Stationary Draw

The stationary draw guides the solo canoe *to* the paddle side. It and its counterpart – the cross draw – are static techniques; they depend on the boat's forward movement to work because neither furnishes any power, only direction. Both work well in their pure form and even better in a slightly modified version in which the paddle blade is extended farther.

An Important Point (Cause and Effect)

The stationary draw acts like a rudder in the front of the canoe. The canoe turns in the direction the blade is pointed or angled.

Details (Modified Version)

Rotate both hands enough to turn the blade up on edge with the power face in toward the hull. Put the blade in the water near the bow at about a 30- to 45-degree angle with both the keel and the water. You may find it necessary to brace the shaft of the paddle against the gunwale. This isn't recommended or necessary if you have enough lower-hand wrist control. The blade will be about half or three-fourths submerged. Keep your lower hand above the gunwale, palm in. Your upper hand is thumbs down, about chest high, and outboard of the

The outward angle on the blade-leading edge of the "standard" stationary draw acts as a brace and rudder to turn the canoe.

The entire blade acts as a rudder and brace on the "modified" stationary draw. Note the upper-hand thumb-down position. This is reversed on a cross-stationary draw.

gunwale. If you don't feel pressure on the blade the boat won't turn well; to make it turn, increase the angle until you do feel pressure.

Details ("Pure Version")

Place the paddle in the water slightly ahead of or beside your body and out as far as you can comfortably reach, power face in toward the hull and leading edge of the blade angled outward at about 30 to 45 degrees (this outward angle is what turns you). Keep the paddle as vertical in the water as you can. As in the modified stationary draw, increase this outward blade angle if the boat doesn't turn.

Recovery

For the pure stationary draw, slice the blade out behind you as in the forward stroke recovery. For the modified version, lift the paddle from the water by raising both arms. (Stationary draws are frequently converted to another stroke. In that case, you may want to use an underwater recovery, slicing the paddle through the water into position for the next stroke).

A footnote to the stationary draw: don't use it to steer the canoe in normal paddling. Use it for what it's intended – turning into eddies, tight pivotal movements, shifting position in current, as a brace – but not a substitute for strokes needing both power and direction.

The Sweeps

Sweep strokes are the workhorses of the solo paddler. So-called because the paddle is held at a low angle instead of almost vertical and the blade literally sweeps through the water, these strokes can provide quick turning or pivotal movements combined with either forward power or rapid slowdown, depending on what you're doing or want to do. Modified, reduced, or combined with other strokes, they furnish these same movements, but only to the degree you want.

Sweeps are not inherently powerful strokes because of the distance from the paddle blade to the hull (although reverse quarter sweeps where your stomach and leg muscles are more easily brought into play can be very powerful), but this same distance does provide the turning movement that makes the sweeps so useful. There are two types of sweeps: forward and reverse. Forward sweeps are done by sweeping the paddle back toward the stern of the boat. In reverse

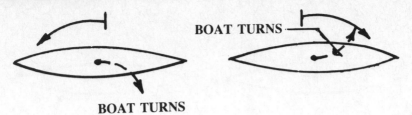

BOAT TURNS

BOAT TURNS

FORWARD   **REVERSE**

THE BASIC FORWARD AND REVERSE SWEEPS

sweeps, the paddle is swept from near the stern forward toward the bow of the boat.

Sweeps may further be categorized into quarter and half forward or reverse sweeps, depending on how much distance the paddle covers in the water. When combined with a cross draw, the half forward sweep actually covers about three-quarters of a circle; in fact it was once known as a three-quarter forward sweep even though the cross draw position of the stroke actually acted as a reverse sweep. Of such contradictions are confused canoeists made! The distinctions are really only necessary for learning the sweeps, but it is a good idea to bear them in mind because they greatly assist in understanding the "how" of some solo maneuvers. Some of these sweeps are shown in the drawing.

Notice there is no reverse equivalent to the combination cross draw/half forward sweep. If you try to do one, you'll end up looking like a corkscrew. You may also notice *all* sweeps do the same thing: turn the canoe. This is true, but the more sweep you do the faster turn you get if all other things such as paddle power remain equal.

Several rules apply to all sweeps. One is: a forward sweep always turns the hull *away* from the paddle side; a reverse sweep always turns it *to* the paddle side. Second: use the power face of the blade on all forward sweeps including the cross draw/half forward combination; use the non-power face on all reverse sweeps except a cross reverse sweep. To ensure this, simply keep the upper paddle hand thumb up in both situations. Third: do not try to follow the gunwale with the paddle stroke. Viewed from above, a sweep covers a full ¼, ½, or ¾ part of a circle.

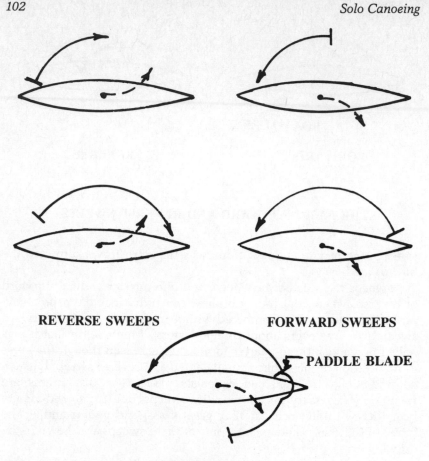

REVERSE SWEEPS   **FORWARD SWEEPS**

PADDLE BLADE

SOME SWEEPS

(BOAT TURNS IN DIRECTION OF DOTTED LINE)

(PADDLE STROKE SHOWN SOLID)

Mechanics of Sweeps

Unlike other paddle techniques in which the paddle is kept more or less perpendicular to the water, thus reducing the stroke's turning effect, a sweep is executed with the paddle angled out at about 30 to 40 degrees or less to the water, which increases its turning ability. This low angle is easy if you just keep your upper hand down about even with your waist when doing the sweep. Place the blade on edge in the water and keep it that way throughout the stroke. Don't totally sub-

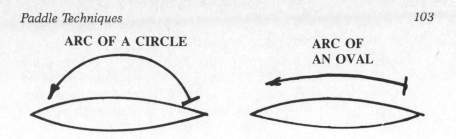

ARC OF A CIRCLE   ARC OF AN OVAL

PATH OF A SWEEP

merge it initially or during the stroke. (This isn't a fine point, it just works out that way.) Start a quarter sweep about even with your hip and sweep toward the bow for a reverse sweep, toward the stern for a forward sweep. In each case, continue the sweep until the blade almost touches the stern (or bow). Start a half forward sweep near the bow, continuing to the stern; start reverse half sweeps near the stern and continue forward to the bow.

Keeping your upper hand down low gives more reach to a sweep.

The Combination Half Forward Sweep/Cross Draw

I term this stroke a sweep because its function is to do exactly what a pure sweep does: turn the canoe while maintaining power on it. It is most commonly used on a maneuver known as the outside pivot turn. It starts with a cross draw (cross strokes are more fully explained elsewhere in this book). The important part here is not to change your grip on the paddle. Swing the paddle across the hull in front of you and, by twisting your body at the waist, put the blade in the water on your off side. The blade edge is perpendicular in the water, the blade partly submerged, and the power face facing forward (your upper-hand thumb will be up). Sweep the blade forward toward the bow as in a reverse sweep and, without contacting the boat, slice the blade out edgeways, "jump" the hull, and put the blade in the water on your on side. The rest of the stroke is a forward half sweep. This stroke will be awkward at first, but it's a good one to know because it combines quick turning without a great deal of loss in power.

Recovery

Recovery on all sweeps is done by lowering the upper hand toward the gunwale and slightly lifting with the lower hand. This slices the paddle blade out edgeways. Feather on recovery by turning the upper-hand thumb away from you toward the bow, upper-hand palm upward. This puts the paddle power face up and applies to both forward and reverse sweeps.

Practicing Steering Strokes

Pick out some stationary object on or near the river such as a tree or a rock, and try to get the canoe to it in a straight line, using only the stroke you're practicing and not resorting to ruddering between strokes. Use a minimum of force in your strokes and concentrate on technique instead of on getting there fast. At first you'll probably overdo everything—overcorrect then have to correct for the over-correction, or sweep each time after a forward correction stroke, for example. Practice will take care of that.

After you get the basics down, start adding some variety. Put a little sweep in your forward stroke and watch how the boat turns faster. Pour on the correction in your forward correction stroke, your J, or your C stroke. You'll find you can actually turn the boat *to* your paddle side this way. Then, after you've got the technique down, in-

The combination half forward sweep/cross draw effectively pivots the canoe.

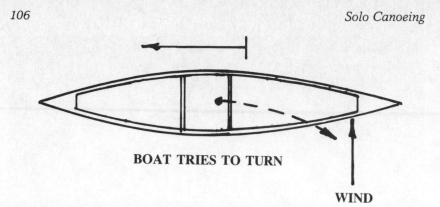

BOAT TRIES TO TURN

WIND

USING THE WIND

crease your force and practice keeping a steady rhythm and length to your paddle strokes while varying the amount of force in the forward and correction parts of it. Above all, watch your paddle blade and its direction of force. Make sure it's on its *edge* for the beginning and end of the C and the end of the forward-correction strokes, and that the correction force is straight *in* or straight *out*.

One thing to remember is that you do not necessarily have to put a correction on *every* stroke to steer the canoe. The wind blowing against your off-paddle side, for example, may furnish the correction power, and you may need to use only a basic forward stroke, balancing its tendency to turn the canoe *into* the wind against the force of the wind.

Going Backward

Backstrokes are used to slow the canoe down when you're going forward or, current permitting, to stop or to back up the river. Besides being useful in various maneuvers, they can offer you a little more thinking time if you find yourself being swept into some situation for which you are unprepared, and, if thinking doesn't help, the back-strokes are useful to reduce the impact!

There are eight basic ways of applying back power or control to your solo canoe: three basic backstrokes, three correction backstrokes, and the reverse sweep and cross reverse sweep (cross draw). The scull can also apply back power as well as some steering, but is not as powerful as the other methods. All these various strokes steer the boat to one degree or the other simply because they all move the hull one way or the other, although only the correction backstrokes can be considered as actually steering the canoe. In real river life, however, you will probably use the reverse sweep and cross reverse sweep most frequently.

The Basic Backstrokes

You do backstroke techniques exactly as you do forward strokes except the power is directed in the opposite direction. All the requirements for effective blade use apply: paddle essentially perpendicular to the water, blade face perpendicular to the keel, stroke done parallel to the keel and not along the arc of the gunwale, face of the blade always as square with the direction of desired force as you can get it.

Backstrokes usually require more power than forward strokes because you're generally contending with the current's efforts to push the canoe downstream. Therefore, the weight and strength of your torso are more frequently needed and used. When using them you are usually in your normal upright position at the beginning of the stroke, but as your paddle moves toward the bow, you may lean back slightly, throwing your weight into the pull of the upper arm. In all basic backstrokes, you will probably find it easier and more natural to keep the paddle more vertical in the water than it was in the forward stroke.

An Important Point (Cause and Effect)

All methods of the basic backstrokes turn the boat *to* your paddle side.

Details: Backstroke Number 1

In the photo, notice that method 1 of the backstroke is done with the hands and paddle in exactly the same position as for the forward stroke. The only difference is that the force of the backstroke will be exerted by the *non-power* face of the blade. Put the blade in the water behind your hip. Both your upper and lower arms will be slightly bent at the elbows. Keep the hand, wrist, and forearm of your lower arm in a straight line so that you can get the most "push" and control out of your lower arm.

Simultaneously push with the lower arm and pull with the upper arm, remembering to keep the stroke parallel with the keel. Continue the stroke on by you, and cut off the power part of it about even with your knee. Your lower arm will become extended during the stroke,

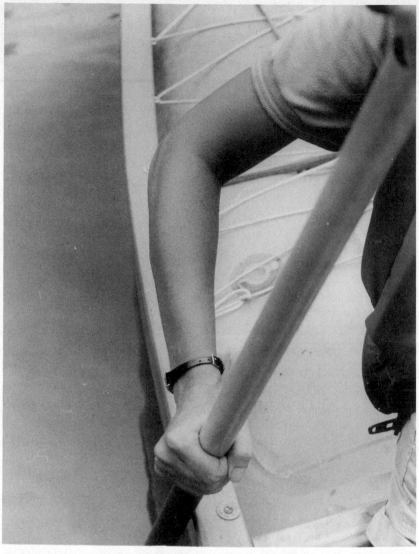

Hand, wrist, and forearm alignment insure the most effective power to the paddle shaft.

but you'll almost immediately start to flex your upper arm, bending it at the elbow and bringing it back toward your paddle-side shoulder. If you've kept the correct paddle-vertical-to-the-water position, this upper hand will be about even with the end of your shoulder or a few inches out beyond both it and the gunwale. If you need the extra power of your body, start the stroke the same way, but as you begin the pushing and pulling with your arms, also begin to lean back with your body weight. Do this smoothly to avoid causing the boat to pitch forward and backward. Time your lean so it's over at the same time as the power part of your stroke. Straighten up at the end of the stroke during the recovery. For even greater power, you can lean forward at the beginning of the stroke and then lean backward during the power part of the pull. This gives you a greater reach and a longer power stroke as well as better using your body muscles and weight. I should add that current theories of biomechanics recommend just the opposite and suggest leaning back at the beginning and forward at the end. Personally, I find this awkward and straining. You might try both ways and adopt the one that works best for you.

Recovery: Method 1

Recovery is above the water. Relax your arms at the end of the power stroke, and bring your upper hand in toward your body and down toward the hull. This will slice the blade out of the water edgeways. Twist both hands forward until the blade is feathered, non-power face down.

Swing your paddle back toward the starting position of a new backstroke. Your upper hand will be at about waist level during this recovery swing. At the end of the swing, just as the blade enters the water, begin bringing the upper arm up in the pull of another backstroke.

Details: Backstroke Number 2

The only differences between method 1 and method 2 of doing the backstroke are the position of the upper arm and hand and the use of the power face rather than the non-power face of your blade for the second method. Method 2 arm position is much stronger, however, as it allows you to use your biceps in the power part of the stroke. Do not change your paddle grip to arrive at this position.

A glance at the photographs of methods 1 and 2 will show you the difference in the upper arm position of the two ways. Simply twist your upper-hand thumb inboard and back toward your face until the palm of your hand is facing you and the power face of your paddle is toward the bow of the canoe. As you twist the paddle with your upper hand, relax the grip of your lower hand and allow the paddle throat to

Rotating the paddle to get the bicep into play increases the available force on backstroke method 2.

rotate in your palm. (Note: This is one of the few times you do not keep a firm grip on the paddle with both hands at all times.) Then reach behind you with the blade and begin the stroke.

The greatest strength in this stroke comes from correct arm position. Align the hand, wrist, and forearm of the lower arm directly behind the paddle shaft; don't have your wrist bent. A common error is to have the upper-arm elbow cocked up in the air. Don't do this. Get your forearm aligned with the paddle shaft and close in behind it so when you flex your muscle you're pulling on the grip.

Recovery: Method 2

Take the blade out of the water edgeways by bringing your upper hand straight across in front of you and down toward the gunwale on the upper-hand side. Stop about even with your upper-hand shoulder. Lift with the lower hand. Do not change hand or paddle position if you are immediately going to do another method 2 backstroke; just swing the blade to the rear and into the water. If you want to feather or go to another stroke, rotate the upper hand thumb forward and outboard, let the paddle slide in your loosened lower-hand grip, and recover as for the forward stroke.

Details: Backstroke Number 3 (Compound Backstroke)

The compound backstroke is somewhat of a cross between the first two methods in that the stroke begins by using the power face of the paddle and ends using the non-power face. Do not change your paddle grip to do this stroke. Twist to your paddle side and lean and reach back, putting the blade in the water as near the stern as possible, the power face toward the bow, the blade perpendicular to the keel, and the entire paddle as vertical in the water as you can get it. Your upper arm will be above your head, knuckles to the stern, your lower arm nearly straight.

Push with your upper arm, pull with your lower one, and simultaneously rotate your body to bring the stroke toward the bow parallel to the keel. Halfway through the stroke (about even with your body), smoothly and quickly rotate the paddle by turning your upper-hand thumb outboard so the non-power face is toward the bow. Push the blade on toward the bow as far as you can comfortably reach.

Recovery: Method 3

Bring your upper hand down in front of you across the canoe and lift with the lower hand. This slices the blade out edgeways. Rotate your upper hand toward the bow to feather the blade.

The Correction Backstrokes

Steering your solo canoe backward may result in a little mental anguish and frustration at first as, in effect, you have to do some backward thinking. Actually, however, it's a simple process of adding some part of correction to either or both ends of any of your basic backstrokes. For the sake of instruction, I've designated these combinations by number.

An Important Point (Cause and Effect)

Backstroke correction number 1 corrects the boat by turning the bow *to* your paddle side. Backstroke correction number 2 corrects the boat by turning the bow *away* from your paddle side. Backstroke correction number 3 first turns the bow to your paddle side then away from it. For the most effective use of any of these corrections, you must balance the force between the correction and the back parts of your stroke, just as you would in a forward-correction stroke.

Details: All Methods

For correction method 1, twist to your paddle side and lean back, placing the blade in the water as near the stern and as far back as you can comfortably reach. The blade will be a few inches out from the hull, parallel to the keel, with the power face toward the hull. Your upper-hand knuckles will be outboard, your upper-hand thumb toward the stern. Push straight out with your lower arm about a foot (this is the correction part of the stroke), then – still pushing – turn the paddle by rotating your upper-hand thumb outboard until the blade is in position for backstroke 1. Use the non-power face throughout the stroke. The remainder of the stroke and the recovery are the same as for backstroke number 1.

For correction method 2, twist to your paddle side even more and place the paddle in the water with the blade on edge, out as far from the hull and as far back toward the stern as you can comfortably reach. Your hands will be in the same position as for method 1. Pull *straight* in (a common error is to throw a little forward stroke in here) with both arms and, as you pull, rotate your upper-hand thumb in toward your

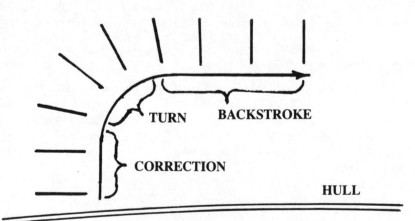

CORRECTION BACK STROKE ONE

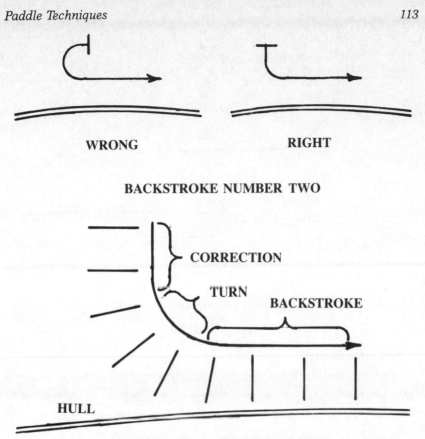

WRONG   **RIGHT**

BACKSTROKE NUMBER TWO

CORRECTION

TURN   BACKSTROKE

HULL

CORRECTION BACKSTROKE TWO

face, relax your lower-hand grip to let the paddle shaft rotate in your hand, and go into backstroke number 2. Use the power face throughout the stroke. The remainder of the stroke and the recovery are the same as for backstroke 2.

For correction method 3, simply do a reverse C stroke, starting off as in method 2 with a pull *in* toward the hull, followed by a back stroke parallel to the keel using the power face. Halfway through the stroke, rotate the blade as in backstroke method 3 (putting the nonpower face toward the bow), continue to the end of the stroke, and end with a push outward, still using the non-power face.

Recovery is done by bringing the upper arm either forward or backward. This slices the blade out on its edge. Feather by rotating the upper hand outboard and forward, thumb outboard.

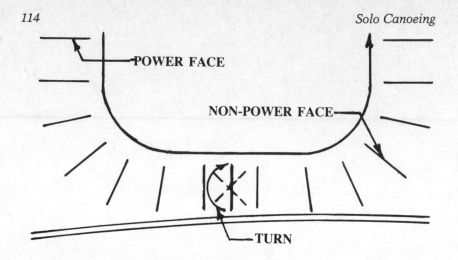

POWER FACE

NON-POWER FACE

TURN

BACKSTROKE NUMBER THREE

The Reverse Sweep

This has already been described under Sweeps. The reverse sweep turns the boat *to* your paddle side faster than the backstrokes, but has less pure backing power.

The Cross Reverse Sweep

This will be described under Cross Strokes in the next chapter. Cross reverse sweeps turn the boat *away* from your normal paddle side and *to* the cross side. Like any sweep, they have greater turning capacity but less power than a stroke done closer to the hull.

Sculling

There are two methods of sculling a canoe; one is the time-honored way of fishermen who use a figure 8 blade motion, the other a simple forward and back motion with the paddle. Either will move the boat to or from the paddle side depending upon the blade angle. The one described here is used most in solo canoeing.

To move *to* your paddle side, place the blade in the water beside your body, paddle vertical and a comfortable distance from the canoe hull. Angle the leading edge of the blade away from the canoe and push the paddle forward (parallel to the keel) in a straight line in whatever length is not awkward for you. At the end of the forward push, turn the blade so the trailing edge is away from the canoe and pull the paddle back to its starting position, then on behind it a distance equal to the forward part of the stroke. Continue doing this and you will pull the boat *toward* the paddle. This is called a sculling draw.

To push the hull *away* from the paddle side, move the paddle in closer to the hull and do exactly the same thing except reverse the blade angle: turn the leading edge in toward the canoe on the forward part of the stroke and the trailing edge in on the back part of the stroke. This is called a sculling pushaway.

Holding the boat steady and straight to the side, counteracting the effects of wind or current, is done by modifying the blade angle and the relative length of the back and forward parts of the stroke. To move

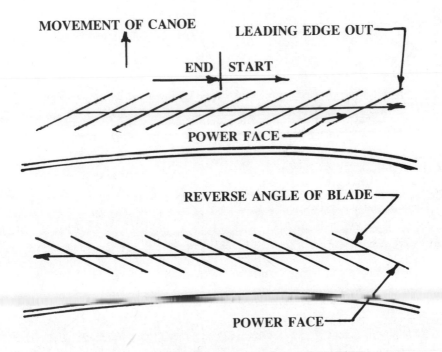

THE SCULLING DRAW

REVERSE ALL BLADE ANGLES FOR THE SCULLING DRAW

the canoe diagonally, either forward or backward using the scull, increase the length of the half stroke in the direction you want to go and decrease the other half of the stroke or do the entire stroke more to the rear or front of your body. To move the boat rearward, for example, twist your body to the paddle side and do the sculling stroke as far behind you as you can comfortably reach.

6

More Paddle Techniques

Moving the Canoe Sideways: Draws and Pries

The two basic strokes for moving a canoe directly to the side are the draw and the pry. Both are strong, effective strokes used when avoiding obstacles, when sudden changes of direction are required, and when time and distance to an obstruction are not plentiful. The strokes can also be used for course correction to steer a canoe down a river; however, they are awkward for this use.

Draws move the boat to your paddle side and may be done directly to the side or diagonally to the rear or to the front. These diagonal draws combine back or forward power and movement with the side movement. Pries push the boat (or one end of it) away from your paddle side. You can do them directly to the side, or toward the bow or the stern. Those done toward the bow or stern are sometimes referred to as shallow-water pries. Their paddle position is different from those done directly to the side of the paddler, and so is their effect on the boat.

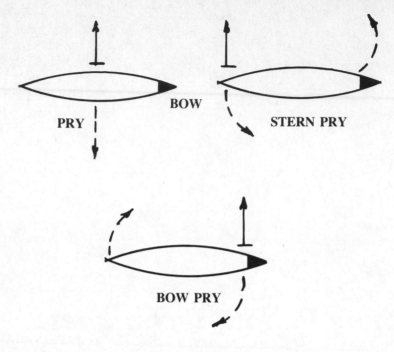

SOME PRIES

An Important Point (Cause and Effect)

A draw always moves the boat *to* your paddle side. A pry always moves it *away* from your paddle side although the boat may pivot. Pure draws or pries (done directly to your side) have little or no turning effect on the boat.

The Draw

In addition to moving the canoe, the draw relieves part of the weight on the hull by letting you temporarily put part of *your* weight on the blade. This not only makes the draw itself more effective, as the canoe is lighter and reacts easier, but also has another important use, which you'll discover when you start doing eddy turns and peel offs. There is one important psychological factor to doing an effective draw: always see yourself planting your paddle firmly in the water and then *pulling the canoe over to the stationary paddle.* This is the object of a draw: to move the canoe to the side. Never look at it as pulling the paddle to the canoe, for that is not the object.

Arm position is important in a draw for both reach and effectiveness. The lower arm should be fully extended and the upper arm stretched out as far as it will reach so the paddle is as near vertical as you can get it when its blade is in the water. To get this correct upper-arm position, grip the paddle with both hands as you would normally hold it while paddling, then swing your outstretched arms straight up over your head so the paddle is parallel to the ground. Now try to swing the paddle over to what would be your paddle side. The upper arm will, of course, hit your head. Shift your upper arm forward just enough to clear your head and you have the right position.

A pure draw is done straight out to the side, with the paddle in line with your hip and shoulder and the blade out as far as you can reach. The paddle is as perpendicular to the water as you can get it (although, in reality, it will most often be diagonal to the plane of the water's surface), and the power face of the blade is facing you and parallel to the keel. The blade should be completely or almost completely buried in the water.

Use your knees and hips to lean the canoe toward the paddle side.

The basic draw position is out beside the hip with the arms extended.

This is much easier to do if you have thigh straps or a saddle. The straps and saddle also allow you to shift your weight and lean the hull without leaning on the gunwale or hanging out over it, although those will work if you have sufficient pressure on the blade to hold the transferred weight. However, don't try this posture until you've practiced and developed confidence in the milder draws.

A powerful draw will support part of your weight, so in drawing literally lean on the paddle. The harder you pull, the more weight it will support, and it won't take you long to discover just how much pull it takes to hold up how much weight! The amount that can be supported also depends on how much of your paddle blade is in the water and how perpendicular your paddle is. The more perpendicular the paddle, the more blade that must be in the water to provide the force to hold the weight up. Less blade in the water means that your paddle must be at more of an angle to provide support. It's best to submerge your paddle blade completely and get the paddle as perpendicular as possible.

Pull in with the lower arm while pushing out and down with the upper arm. Straighten your body as the canoe is pulled closer to the paddle. Keep the paddle as perpendicular to the water throughout the stroke as you can and maintain the force of the draw straight in toward your hip. Maintain the face of the blade perpendicular to the force of your pull; in this case, with the face parallel to the keel. As you pull in, simultaneously bring your body back in the boat smoothly and evenly, transferring your weight from the blade to the hull.

Cut the power of your stroke off about six inches before the paddle strikes the hull of the canoe. Your body should now be back in the canoe and your weight off the blade. If you let the paddle come on in and touch the hull, it's likely to hang there, especially in current. This unexpected "hanging" or a sudden current push on the flat of the blade could dump you or snatch the paddle out of your hands.

Recovery

Recovery on a draw is to the rear and above or in the water. For an above-water recovery, slice the edge-up paddle out behind you by bringing your upper hand down toward the gunwale and keeping your lower arm extended. Do not lift the paddle to remove it from the water. Rotate your upper-hand thumb out and away from you so the power face of the paddle is up and parallel to the water, and swing the paddle back out in this feathered position. During the swing, turn the power face back over toward you by rotating your upper-hand thumb back. Simultaneously, start lifting your upper arm back into its over-the-head position so that by the time the swing is completed, the paddle is back in position for another draw.

For an underwater recovery, simply turn the blade so the power face is toward the stern (your upper-hand thumb rotates away from you and outboard) — which is the recommended way — or the power face is forward (upper-hand thumb rotated toward you and inboard), which many find easier, and slice back to your starting position.

Important Points and Practice of the Draw

Remember that the more weight you lean on your paddle, the stronger must be your draw; also, you cannot maintain your initial posture of hanging far out over the gunwale to the end of the stroke or you'll find yourself leaning over a vertical paddle blade that offers no support. Practice will soon teach you how far out you can reach with what paddle angle and when to get your body weight off the paddle and back in the canoe. After a few spills you'll begin to discover the various correct blends of weight, lean, power, and timing.

The Pry

A stroke often taught in lake canoeing is called a pushaway. Although it is intended to do the same thing as a pry, it's important for you to distinguish the difference between the two. The pushaway is just what it says: you push the face of the blade away from the side of the canoe. Try it and you'll find that it's a weak stroke even though you can keep the paddle vertical and exert all your force to the side. A pry, on the other hand, is just what it says: you are prying the boat to the side, using the principles of leverage, which, while forcing you to sacrifice length of effective stroke, greatly multiplies the force within that length. The pry is a powerful, effective stroke, albeit a short one; the pushaway is not.

The pure pry is done beside the knee, not the shoulder, and there is no diagonal component. It uses the bilge and gunwale as a fulcrum and the paddle shaft just rocks up and down them. In theory the shaft does not lose contact with the boat; in practice you will find that it sometimes does because it's difficult to do a sequence of rapid pries and keep contact all the time. The secret to learning (and using) the pry is smoothness and rhythm. Learn the motion first, then gradually apply power.

You may need to slide your lower hand up the shaft enough for your fingers to clear the gunwale slightly when the paddle is in position for the pry. Twist to your paddle side and put the power face of the blade as flat as you can against the bilge of the boat and parallel to the keel. The blade is totally submerged and usually part of the throat is also. Fully extend your upper arm so your upper hand is well out over the water.

Apply a lot of power from the very beginning of the stroke and all the way through it; otherwise, the pry loses much of its effectiveness. This, of course, does not apply when you are first learning it. Roll the throat and shaft of the paddle smoothly up the side of the boat by pulling inboard on the upper hand. Keep the paddle shaft in contact with the hull at all times. It is not a good idea to maintain boat and shaft contact by clamping the paddle to the gunwale with your lower-hand fingers or thumb. Although this is often done, it encourages a lack of development of lower-wrist control and is also a good way to severely pinch fingers. It also gives you a weak grip on the paddle. Maintain the contact with lower-hand wrist action alone. Continue to "roll" the paddle up until the shaft touches the gunwale. Note that your total stroke travel is only about 12 to 16 inches long. At this point your upper hand will be about in line with your chin if you're in the center of the boat. This is the place to stop the stroke; beyond this point the blade begins to lift water, exerting more upward than sideways force. If you don't cut the stroke off here, your effort is merely pulling the gunwale down instead of doing its job of prying the canoe sideways. The whole stroke is short but must be rapid, powerful, and rhythmical.

Recovery

Recovery is done underwater. Rotate the paddle by turning your upper-hand thumb out and away from you; this will put the blade face perpendicular to the keel and the power face facing you. Rock the blade back under the canoe to the bilge by pushing out with the upper hand. Firmly hold the shaft in contact with the canoe hull with the lower hand and bend the lower-hand wrist to allow these twists of the paddle. Do not loosen your lower-hand grip and let the paddle shaft slip through your hand as it twists. Keep a firm grip with both hands at all times. Just before the edge of the blade strikes the bilge, turn your upper-hand thumb back toward your face and, as the blade flattens out, bring its power face against the bilge once more.

The start of the pry: blade under the bilge, body rotated, upper arm straight, lower hand above gunwale.

The end of the pry. The paddle shaft is still in contact with the boat. Stop pulling about halfway across the hull.

If you need to, you are then ready to immediately go into another pry stroke. All this is done in one smooth, continuous motion. The strokes are short, rapid, and powerful, and the recovery must also be smooth and rapid. Doing a pry is sort of four-part rhythm – pull, turn, recover, turn; pull, turn, recover, turn. Practicing slowly at first and gathering speed and power as you develop coordination will help you learn the pry.

Variations on the Draw

You will probably have occasion to maintain some forward or backward power on the boat and simultaneously move it sideways, or to move the boat diagonally. Diagonal draws are one simple way to do this, as they easily blend in with other strokes.

To do a diagonal draw to the rear, twist to your paddle side and place the paddle in the water behind you and away from the boat as far as you can reach. Be sure the blade is square with the way you want the boat to go. Your arms will be fully extended. Now pull in diagonally toward your body as in a normal draw. To recover, lower the upper hand toward the gunwale and slice the blade out edgeways. A diagonal draw to the bow is done exactly the same except you'll lean forward and pull toward you from the front of the boat.

Variations on the Pry

The stern pry and the bow pry (both also called shallow-water pries) are the two basic variations of the pure pry. The stern pry turns the bow *to* the paddle side; the bow pry turns the bow *away* from the paddle side. The mechanics of both are simple but completely different from the standard pry.

— MOVEMENT —

TO REAR   TO FRONT

SOME DRAW VARIATIONS

The Stern Pry

The stern pry is little more than the correction part of the forward correction stroke. Position the blade on its edge, power face toward the hull and close to the stern of the canoe. Your upper hand should be about a foot above the gunwale, thumb up, and your lower hand above the gunwale and about even with your hip. Now pry off the gunwale by pulling in with your upper hand. Do not push with your lower hand. This will turn the boat. If you continue the swing of the pry you'll be converting to a reverse sweep, which will turn the boat but also slow it down – something you may or may not want to do.

The Bow Pry

The bow pry paddle position is the same as for the stern pry except the blade is angled forward, toward the bow. The power face is still in toward the hull so your upper hand is thumbs down. This pry may easily be converted into a forward sweep, which turns the boat and also adds forward power. The bow pry's greatest use is in course correction of the bow when you're paddling backward.

The correct position of the paddle for a stern pry. The technique is very useful for quick angle-setting or to start inside pivot turns.

The bow pry pushes the bow away from the paddle side.

Holding the Canoe Up

You'll use two basic paddle techniques to steady, support, or bring a solo canoe back upright when it's trying to roll. These techniques are called braces. One, the low brace, is used when the canoe is rolling *to* your paddle side. The other, the high brace, is used when the canoe is rolling *away* from your paddle side. Braces are also a vital part of eddy turns and peel offs, as you'll learn in the chapter on maneuvers, and the low brace, in a modified form, is often used as a slowing and/or steadying technique in rough water, in which case it is usually called a "trailing" brace. This is described under variations of the low brace.

The High Brace

A high brace is nothing but a draw, without the actual drawing motion toward the canoe. You're simply "catching" the water with the blade to stop the boat's rolling. Insert the paddle in the water exactly as you would for a draw—power face in toward the hull, blade parallel to the keel, both arms extended, paddle close to vertical in the water, and all done out beside your shoulder. Because a high brace is used to stop the boat rolling *away* from the paddle, pressure on the blade is created by the rolling motion itself. On the river it's rarely possible for you to put any additional pressure on the blade, as both the boat and you are usually already off balance and tilted *away* from the paddle before the blade enters the water.

The Low Brace

The low brace does two things. It provides a surface against which to exert force when you need to push the canoe back upright, and this same surface also gives you a platform on which to rest part of your weight while you're using the brace. Relieving part of the weight on the canoe, of course, makes it roll back up easier.

Low braces require more faith in the paddle than do high braces. This is the greatest difficulty in learning the technique. It is essential, however, you develop this faith that the blade will support part of your weight, and get out and *lean* on the paddle. How much it will support depends upon a number of factors and is something you can only learn by experience – and by falling in until you gain that experience!

A high brace in action. The canoe is in a small hydraulic.

The low brace. In the current, an up angle on the blade's leading edge keeps it from diving on you.

Paddle Position

In a pure brace the entire length of the paddle is completely outboard the canoe, parallel or nearly parallel to the surface of the water, and below the sheer line of the canoe. The brace is done out beside your hip or at a point roughly between your hip and knee on the paddle side.

Body and Hand Position

Do not change your normal paddling grip with either hand. Twist to the paddle side and lay the entire paddle flat on the water and perpendicular to the keel, the grip end toward the hull, the blade flat on the surface, *non-power face down.* To do this you will have to lean out over the gunwale. In a really strong brace your body may even be hung out over the gunwale. For practice, get your hip up against the gunwale and *lean!* Align the lower hand, wrist, and forearm in a straight line.

A brace that failed!

Put your weight (or part of it) directly over your lower hand. Don't be afraid of falling; the low brace requires confidence and will never be effective until you have that confidence.

Your upper-hand knuckles will be in the water so your palm is up and your lower hand will be palm down and the knuckles facing the bow. This hand position is very important; it allows you to use your biceps on the "pull." In addition you just can't effectively pull up very far with your upper palm down. Try it and you'll see. As the blade touches the water and your weight bears down on the lower hand, pull up very strongly with your upper hand. Do all this simultaneously and swiftly. If done correctly, the lever effect of the blade on the water will push against the water surface and push the boat upright. If you hesitate too long, the blade will sink, and you with it!

Recovery

Emphasis must be on the timing of the end of the brace and the withdrawal of your weight back into the canoe and off the blade. You should begin to pull your body weight back in near the end of the lift and push of your arms. Don't "paddle" back in by dragging the blade through the water. Brace and come off of it so you can almost immediately lift the paddle from the water for another low brace if you need it.

Variations and Other Uses

While learning you should do the low brace as outlined above; on the river you'll brace from any position you can! When low bracing in choppy water or waves, keep a slight up angle on the leading edge of the blade to prevent it from diving on you. When bracing in frothy water, your blade may (in fact, probably will) vanish below the froth until it finds "solid" water to rest on. In this case your whole paddle and both your hands may be completely submerged. In very frothy water the water may be too "thin" to support a brace at all.

Another use for the low brace is as a third point of support in rough water; this is known as a trailing brace. Trail the paddle behind you at about a 45-degree angle to the keel, non-power face down. In this use your upper hand is usually inboard, and the paddle is at about 30 degrees to the water instead of horizontal. Exert more or less pressure on the blade to slow down or gain extra support. Be sure to keep a slight up angle on the leading edge.

Practice of the Low Brace

A good confidence builder is to practice low braces in shallow water where the bottom will catch your blade if your brace fails. You can also try dipping the gunwale of the boat, taking in water, and bringing the boat back up with the brace. Try varying the amount of weight, force, lean, and timing until you arrive at what you can do under various conditions. You'll find that under some conditions you can lean on the brace a relatively long time. This becomes easier and more effective the greater speed differential there is between the boat and the current. Practice will show you what you can and can't do. To be effective, braces must be done automatically. If you have to stop to think which brace to use, it is usually too late! Practice of the bracing stroke will get the technique down, but only experience can make bracing instinctive.

Cross Strokes

Cross strokes are paddle strokes done on the opposite side of the canoe from your normal paddle side, but done *without* changing hand position on the paddle. The paddle is simply swung across the boat and into the water while you maintain your original hand grip. Many paddlers have difficulty comprehending this distinction between cross strokes and swapping paddle sides (in which you *do* change hand grips), but it is an important one. Cross strokes are used as a matter of convenience and expediency generally when you wish to make some movement to your off side that requires or can be expedited by a quick paddle technique or stroke or two on that side. It's much faster and easier to do a cross stroke than to swap sides and then swap back. In fact, you'll find that often you won't have time to do such swapping, and it's then that the cross strokes really prove their usefulness. Cross strokes may feel a little awkward at first, as the body has to be twisted at the waist toward the side of the stroke.

In theory (and if you were flexible enough) almost any stroke could be done as a cross stroke to one degree or another. In practice, only a few are commonly used: the cross high brace, cross reverse sweep, and cross stationary draw. Cross draws and cross back strokes are used occasionally, and now and again you'll have need of a cross

The basic cross stroke position. A combination of waist twist and arm movement keeps the upper-arm elbow low – where it should be!

forward stroke. Some of these cross strokes are not as effective as their on-side counterparts, but all are useful and necessary to the solo paddler. All require practice to make them as efficient and natural as possible. Probably the best way to practice cross strokes is to first do a few forward strokes each time then go into the cross position.

Note: In each of the following descriptions of the various cross strokes, remember that the sentences below precede *all* further instructions:

Without changing either hand position on the paddle or letting the paddle rotate in the lower hand, swing the paddle across the hull to your off side. Do this by a combination of arm motion and twisting your body at the waist. Lift the paddle only enough to clear the gunwales.

Cross High Brace

Go through the basic motions. Continue turning the paddle and twisting your body and upper-hand wrist until the flat of the blade is

The cross high brace.

Cross high brace recovery to the "on" side.

parallel to the keel, power face in toward the boat, and as straight out from your body as your flexibility will allow. Extend your arms so the entire paddle is as vertical as possible in the water and as far out away from the hull as you can stretch, just as you would in an on-side high brace. *Your upper-hand thumb will be pointing forward, the palm down toward the water.* All the principles of a normal on-side high brace now apply. Recovery is done by bringing the upper hand down toward the gunwale. This slices the blade out edgeways in *front* of you (just opposite to an on-side brace).

Cross Reverse Sweep

Go through the basic motions. This stroke is exactly like the first part of the combination half forward sweep/cross draw, except start it as far behind you as you can. Remember the low angle of the paddle in a sweep and keep your upper hand down about even with your chest or stomach. Put the blade in the water as far behind you as you can with the blade edge approximately perpendicular to the water and the

The start of a cross reverse sweep. Note the low upper-arm position and the body twist.

power face forward. The upper-hand thumb is up, palm facing forward. Sweep forward toward the bow but do not contact the hull with the blade.

For recovery, lift the paddle from the water edgeways. This is such a short stroke no feathering of the blade is really needed. For recovery to your on-side, lift the paddle high enough to clear the gunwales. Rotate the upper hand so the power face is down toward the hull as you swing the paddle across the boat.

Cross Stationary Draw

This is a very useful cross technique for solo boating. The paddle blade acts as a rudder to turn the boat in the direction the blade points.

Go through the basic motions. Put the blade in the water as you would for an on-side stationary draw except with your upper-hand thumb up and the palm facing inward. This puts the power face in toward the hull. The upper hand will be over toward your off side and about chest high, the entire paddle at about 30 to 45 degrees to the

A modified cross stationary draw. The upper hand is in the thumb-up position.

keel, and the blade edgeways in the water. The throat or lower shaft of the paddle may be braced against the gunwale. If you don't feel water pressure on the blade (or the boat doesn't turn), increase the blade angle. Note that you don't have to brace against the gunwale if you can control the paddle angle without doing so. In fact, it's better not to brace like that.

For recovery, lift the blade from the water and swing the paddle back across the hull, rotating the upper hand inward toward your face as you do so. The power face is down toward the hull as the paddle crosses the gunwales.

Cross Draw

Go through the basic motions and into the cross high brace position. Draw as you would for an on-side draw, applying weight and pressure to the blade. Do not contact the hull with the blade. Recover as in the cross high brace with the blade slicing out edgeways in *front* of you.

Cross Backstroke

This is a difficult stroke for a lot of paddlers, as it feels extremely awkward, but it's also effective. Cross backstrokes are sometimes useful in maintaining back-ferry angles and controlling the boat when

Some suppleness is called for on an effective cross backstroke. Note that the paddle power face is toward the bow.

you're going backward, although a cross reverse sweep is more commonly used.

Go through the basic motions but continue to twist at the waist until the blade can be put in the water well behind your body. You may need to rotate your legs and knees toward the cross paddle side to do this. The blade edge is perpendicular to the keel, the paddle as perpendicular to the water as you can get it, and both hands outboard. The upper-hand thumb is pointing out, the lower palm facing the rear. The power face is to the front of the boat. Do the backstroke by a combination of arm power and turning your body back toward the center of the hull. All the basic backstroke principles apply during the stroke. For recovery rotate the upper hand inboard to turn the blade on edge, power face in toward the hull, slice the blade out edgeways in front of you, and twist back around for another stroke. To return to the on side, carry the blade back across the hull power face down.

The forward cross stroke – awkward looking but effective!

Cross Forward Stroke

You won't find this in any canoe book I've ever read, but you will see it done on the river. Usually only a few strokes are used. It's rather awkward and not too efficient because of the paddler's position, but it does the job. This is one of the strokes where forward and back body motion is used to add power to the stroke.

Go through the basic motions. Put the blade in the water in front of you about where you would for a normal forward stroke and in the usual forward stroke position (blade edge perpendicular to the keel, entire paddle perpendicular to the water). The upper-hand thumb is in, palm to the rear, blade power face to the rear. Lean forward and, as you stroke, lean back. This is done in short fore and aft bobbing motions. Usually these strokes are rather short in length. To recover for another cross forward stroke, rotate the upper-hand thumb forward, palm inboard, slice the blade out of the water edgeways in front of you, and reach forward again. To recover to your on side, slice the paddle out the same way and swing across the hull power face down.

7

Maneuvers

You already know how to do some maneuvers in the solo canoe, probably more than you think. You can paddle forward and backward, sideslip to either side, and turn gradually or pivot quickly to left or right. These maneuvers require only paddle power on the hull. All of them can be practiced and performed in still water. Most of the maneuvers in this chapter, however, while still requiring paddle power, also require a current. In fact, without moving water, most of them won't work at all. So you might say this chapter is the real dividing line between the still-water canoeist and the river runner.

Paddle Power

As a solo canoeist you have only one source of power in the boat— you! In many river situations it is vital that you be able to simultaneously maintain this power *and* control of the canoe. While this may sound obvious, many beginning solo canoeists just don't do it. Instead they tend to dawdle around applying correction only and in the process lose their position in the river, then try to regain the loss with power strokes without any correction. Even worse, they use strokes for control or correction that directly oppose their intended purpose (using backstrokes in a forward ferry, for example) or drag the paddle in the water to swing the bow around on a forward ferry. None of these (and many other such substitutions for skill) are very effective — as a few crunchings into rocks or sideways rolls over drops soon show!

The point is to develop the ability to use power only, correction only, or simultaneous power and correction; to know when what you're doing is working *for* you and when you're only defeating yourself, and then do what you should be doing. This will all come to you with experience, but some thought will help too.

Pivot Turns (Spins)

It is often desirable in a river to be able to spin your canoe without moving either back or forward. Pivot turns do this. They are done to either your normal paddling side (an inside pivot turn) or opposite your normal paddling side (an outside pivot turn). Both are done by applying paddle strokes you already know (or should, if you haven't skipped the preceding two chapters).

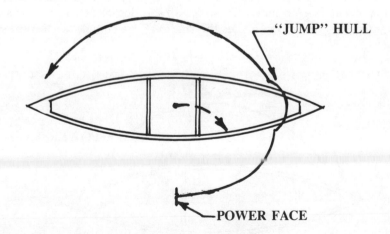

"JUMP" HULL

POWER FACE

THE OUTSIDE PIVOT TURN

Outside Pivot Turns

To spin your canoe in an outside pivot turn, simply do a half forward sweep/cross draw combination as described under Sweeps in Chapter 5. The cross draw begins the swing of your bow away from your normal side; the half forward sweep continues it. How many strokes it takes to make the full 180-degree turn is a product of your muscle and skill and the style of canoe you're in. You may even make it in one stroke. Recovery is the same as for the forward sweep.

Inside Pivot Turns, Method 1

Start with a reverse sweep using the non-power face of the blade. About even with your body (halfway through the stroke), rotate the blade as you would for a combination backstroke, turning the power face toward the bow by rotating your upper-hand thumb toward the stern and down. Continue the arc of the sweep on toward the bow. Recovery may be underwater by slicing your blade edgeways along the length of the canoe to the start of another reverse sweep or another stroke, or by lowering your upper hand enough to lift the blade from the water.

Inside Pivot Turns, Method 2

This method uses a modified C stroke, in which the forward part of the stroke is eliminated. It is a totally underwater stroke. Viewed from the top, the stroke makes the shape of a rectangle with rounded ends.

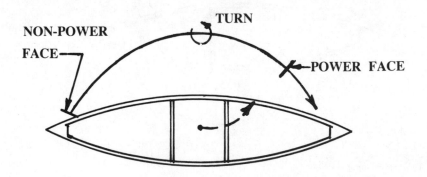

THE INSIDE PIVOT TURN

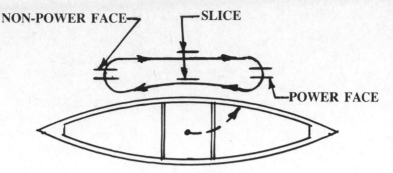

ANOTHER INSIDE PIVOT TURN

Begin your C stroke as usual, pulling straight in toward the hull, but do not turn the blade for the forward stroke part. Instead, bring the blade on in close to the hull, keeping it parallel to the keel, and slice it on its edge through the water back to where you would normally begin your pry. The farther you have the blade under the bilge, the more effective the stroke will be. Now, instead of prying off the gunwale, push *outward* on the paddle with both arms. The blade is still parallel to the keel. When you're at the limit of your arm reach, slice the paddle back through the water to your beginning position. The entire stroke and recovery is underwater and the blade is always parallel to the keel.

For the most effect, keep the paddle perpendicular to the water throughout the stroke, which means keep both hands outboard all the time. During the second correction push, you'll straighten out both arms. Keep them in this position during the recovery. Do not bring your upper hand inboard. For a lesser turn, use the same initial pull and slice, but instead of pushing outward for the second correction, substitute a hard stern pry or correction pry as you would in a normal C stroke.

Other Ways to Turn

The Stationary Draw, Cross Stationary Draw, and Stern Pry

You already know these from the chapters on paddle strokes. This is only a reminder that in the context of this chapter, they all turn the boat one way or the other but without applying any forward or back power.

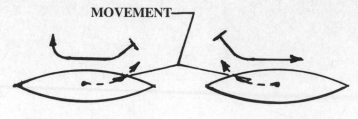

THE "C" STROKE   BACK STROKE

SCULLING   DRAW

SOME DIAGONAL STROKES WITH POWER

Diagonal Strokes

This was mentioned in the paddling chapters in relation to the draw strokes. It also applies here. You will often need to move the canoe diagonally, but keep power on it too. This is a simple matter of modifying your strokes to include the diagonal component. The illustration shows several typical examples. You'll discover others as your experience increases. In each case, of course, the power part of the stroke and the correction part of the stroke must be balanced so the boat moves exactly where you want it to.

Eddy Turns and Peel Offs (Peel Outs)

It's hilarious to onlookers to see a canoeist charge into or out of an eddy and flip right out of the boat. Using eddy turn and peel off techniques would have prevented both the spill and the laughter. These two maneuvers get you from a current into an eddy (an eddy turn) or from an eddy into a current (a peel off or peel out) without your canoe rolling out from under you. As you'll be doing a lot of this on the river, they will probably be the most used and most useful river maneuvers you'll ever learn. They're also a lot of fun to do!

Eddy turn and peel off techniques use the difference in speed and force between the slack water of an eddy and the moving water of the main current to turn the canoe. This same difference, however, is what can also turn the canoe over. There's no problem when the difference is small (a "weak" eddy), as you can just paddle across the eddy line with no more than a slight momentary tilt to the boat. As the differential increases, however, or the eddy line becomes more defined, the canoe begins to roll a little more as you cross this line. The rolling tendency increases with the differential until the canoe finally rolls right out from under you. Eddy turns and peel offs both offset this differential rolling tendency and, at the same time, use it to do most of the work of the technique itself.

An eddy turn works because the bow of the canoe is in the still or

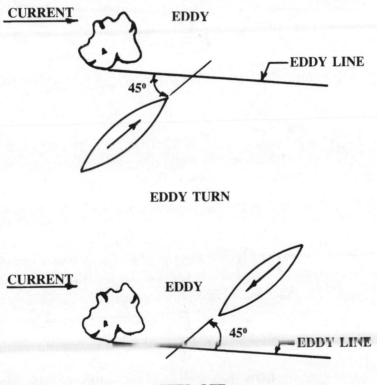

EDDY TURN AND PEEL OFF ANGLES

slow-moving eddy water, while the stern is still exposed to the current and being swung around by it. Thus, you always end up in the eddy facing upstream. A peel off works because the stern is in the eddy and the bow exposed to the current, which swings the bow downstream. The mechanics of eddy turns and peel offs are exactly the same. So, if you can do one, you can do the other. The only difference is the direction you're going when you cross the eddy line – downstream for an eddy turn, upstream for a peel off. Both eddy turn and peel off techniques may be done to your paddle side (on side) or opposite your paddle side (off side). You do *not* need to swap paddle sides!

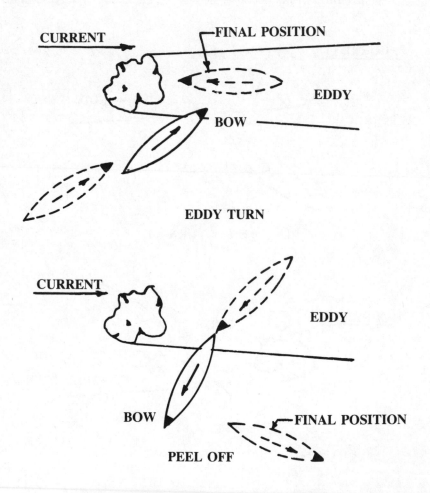

BASIC EDDY TURNS AND PEEL OFFS

The big thing to remember is this: To offset the canoe's rolling, you must lean your weight in the opposite direction and support yourself with a paddle brace. This lean and brace is always to the *inside* of the turn, just like leaning a bicycle around a sharp curve. How much lean and brace depends on the water conditions; the greater the current speed and differential, the more lean it takes.

Duffek Turns

Although either a high brace done toward the bow or a stationary draw will turn and brace the solo canoe in eddy turns and peel offs, a paddle technique known as the Duffek does a more effective job. The Duffek is a combination of four paddle techniques, all done as one continuous stroke. The first three are a stationary draw, a high brace, and a draw done in front of your body toward the bow; these both turn and brace your canoe. The final technique is a forward stroke that provides additional impetus to the hull after the turn is virtually completed. Duffeks turn the canoe more sharply than a brace alone and also maintain forward power on the hull. Note that the *power face* of the blade is used throughout and the blade stays in the water the entire stroke. Recovery is as for the forward stroke.

Eddy Turns

An eddy is strongest at its upstream end, just below whatever is forming the eddy. Eddy turns work best, then, if you get your bow in

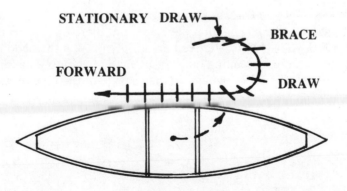

THE DUFFEK TURN

as close downstream of the obstruction as you can. To hit the eddy accurately, you have to allow for the fact that your canoe is moving both downstream and toward the eddy at the same time. It's sort of like hitting a moving target, except in this case the target is still and you're moving.

On-Side Mechanics

Approach the eddy at about a 45-degree downstream angle to the eddy line. Don't start swinging around bow upstream before you get there or you'll be trying to ferry into the eddy instead of doing an eddy turn. Don't drift across the eddy line; power across it maintaining your angle and, as your bow enters the eddy, substitute your Duffek for the next power stroke you would have done had you not intended to eddy out. As your bow crosses the eddy line, lean to the *inside* of the turn and simultaneously do the stationary draw part of the Duffek. This blade work must be in the eddy, else the turn won't work as well and possibly not at all. The brace and lean must also be done just as your bow enters the eddy. If the differential is very large, even a second's delay may roll you over!

The outward angle of the blade on your stationary draw (plus the force differential on the canoe hull) will start the eddy turn. Immediately and smoothly convert to a high brace, then a draw toward the bow (in effect a reverse sweep). All of this assists the boat in its turning, and all of it takes less time to do than it does for you to read this. By now the boat should have almost completed its turn, so you convert to the forward stroke, which pulls you firmly into the eddy and completes the Duffek.

You should feel pressure on the blade as the boat begins to turn. You must have some weight on the blade, put there by leaning into the turn and on your Duffek. Remember, simply putting the paddle blade in the water and *not* leaning on it or, as many beginning paddlers do, by actually shifting their weight to the outside of the turn, is an excel-

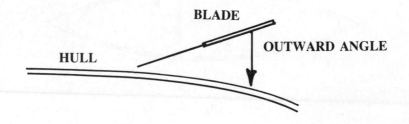

lent way to take an unexpected bath. How much weight and how much lean depends on a lot of things, but this is a product of experience and falling in. You'll be able to better judge after a little of both!

The pressure on the Duffek will lessen as the boat turns and more of it enters the eddy. As the pressure reduces, pull your weight back off the paddle blade and into the boat. Do this smoothly, coordinating the gradual reduction of pressure on the blade with the gradual transfer of weight back into the canoe. In a strong eddy, all this will happen in the first few seconds after your bow crosses the eddy line. This is one reason the maneuver is so enjoyable; you can really be snapped around with very little effort on your part. Always help any turn by using your stomach and leg muscles to "twist" the boat into the turn under you.

Off-Side Mechanics

The only difference in an off-side solo eddy turn is you will do all cross techniques in the eddy: a cross stationary draw, converting to a

The Duffek turn. It's most effective on eddy turns and peel outs.

cross high brace to a cross draw to a cross forward stroke or, to put it more simply, a cross Duffek. You will still lean and brace to the inside of the turn. As the boat turns and the pressure comes off the blade, either do the cross forward stroke of the Duffek to drive you on solidly into the eddy or cross back over to your on side and do a normal forward stroke or sweep. Remember, for a cross stationary draw your upper-hand thumb is up, not down as on the on-side technique.

Peel Offs (Peel Outs)

Peel off techniques are exactly like eddy turns as far as the lean and brace are concerned. In a peel off, however, you are sitting in the eddy and the intent is to paddle out into the current and let it turn you downstream.

Power across the eddy line in an upstream direction of about 45 degrees to the current. As your bow enters the current, lean to the inside of the turn (in this case downstream) and either do a Duffek or the cross techniques described under eddy turns, depending on whether you're doing an on-side or an off-side peel off. The stationary draw is extended toward the bow, the blade on edge and angled out from your keel line, your upper hand thumbs down for an on-side turn, thumb up for an off-side turn. Remember, the lean and brace must be done simultaneously with the bow entering the current; don't delay or you may be swimming!

As the boat turns and the pressure on the blade decreases, shift your weight smoothly back into the canoe. When the turn is complete or nearly so, convert to a forward stroke or a cross forward stroke. Try to twist the boat into the turn with your leg and stomach muscles. Another trick to help you turn faster is to really heel the boat over on your lean; the more lean you have, the faster the boat will turn.

Ferries

Ferries are the magic carpets of river canoeing. They allow you to move sideways in the river to dodge an obstruction, search for a path, or cross a current. Their greatest value is that this is done with no or minimum downstream movement and, because the river itself is doing part of the work for you, it's done with much less effort than trying to paddle across the same path. Ferries are particularly useful when time and distance are short between you and something downstream you wish to avoid.

Ferries work because of a simple relationship between two

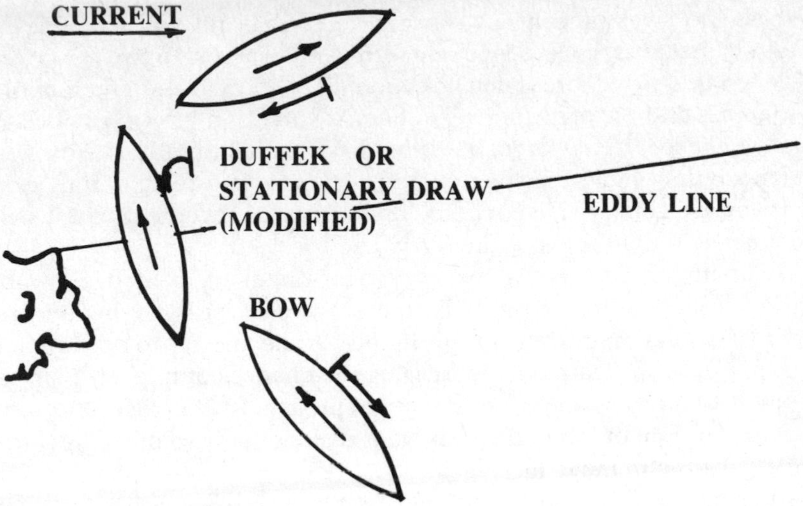

CURRENT

DUFFEK OR
STATIONARY DRAW
(MODIFIED)

EDDY LINE

BOW

ON SIDE

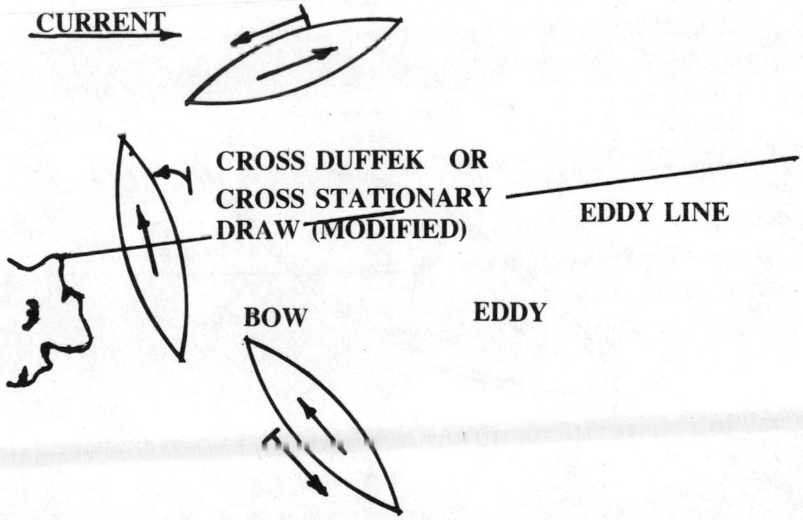

CURRENT

CROSS DUFFEK OR
CROSS STATIONARY
DRAW (MODIFIED)

EDDY LINE

BOW   EDDY

OFF SIDE

PADDLE STROKES IN A PEEL OFF

forces—the river pushing you in one direction and you paddling in another. Because your canoe can't go both ways at once, it moves between these two forces in a direction dictated by the strength of the two forces and the angle between them, a condition known in physics as a *resultant force*. Obviously ferries have their limitations. You will reach a point where the river overpowers you. In a really strong current you are going to have marked downstream movement, but it will be much less than without the ferry.

The illustrations show two ways you might try to dodge an obstruction that's close to you. In both cases you are still moving toward the rock at least at current speed. If you paddle and try to power your way around it, you are only increasing the chances of impact. Using a ferry, however, slows or halts your approach to the rock and also moves you right or left to dodge it; your distance stays almost the same and your time to move increases.

Ferries may be done to the left or right and facing upstream or downstream. If you are facing bow downstream, it is called a back ferry because your paddle power is some sort of backstroke or reverse sweep and your *stern* is angled in the direction you want to go. If facing bow upstream, it's called a forward ferry as your paddle power is some sort of forward stroke or forward sweep and your *bow* is facing the way you want to go. Forward ferries are much easier to control solo,

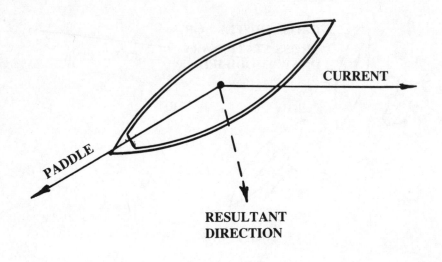

WHY A FERRY WORKS

STEERING

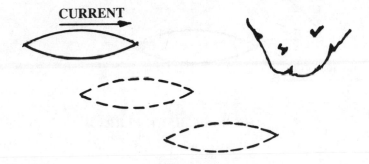

SIDE SLIP

TWO WAYS OF AVOIDING AN OBSTACLE

thus much more used by the solo paddler where long traverses are required. Solo back ferries are usually used only for short, quick sideways movements.

Do remember, however, that with a forward ferry, you must ultimately turn your canoe around and face it bow downstream (or run the entire river backward). Don't pivot into a forward ferry position in some awkward place that will force you to run backward where you don't want to.

The Ferry Angle

A good beginning angle for a ferry is about 30 degrees to the current, but every ferry will be different as the water conditions will always be different. You'll need to adjust your angle once you're into

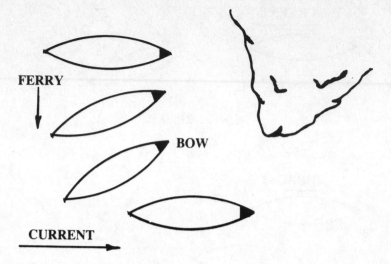

THE BASIC BACK FERRY

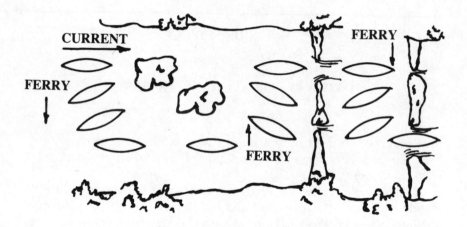

FERRIES IN ACTION

the ferry, and may also need to adjust it during the ferry if the water speed or current direction changes. The angle is really a seat-of-the-pants thing, something you adjust by feel or senses. As a general rule, however, the faster the current, the "sharper" or more parallel to it you need to be. Conversely, in a very slow current, you may flatten out your angle, be almost broadside to it. Once you feel your first ferry, you'll know what you're looking for. Paddle power affects the angle, too; the two are always complimentary. Working them together gives you a choice of actions. A sharp angle lets you paddle less powerfully, but slows your sideways movement. In the same current, a flatter angle speeds up your sideways motion, but you have to paddle harder.

Your angle must be with the current your canoe is *in*. Don't set your angle by watching the shoreline, ledges, rocks, or the current twenty feet away. They can all fool you into thinking you have the right angle where you have the wrong one, or none at all. Finally, it's always a good idea to lean your canoe slightly downstream on *any* ferry.

Control Your Angle

Remember—setting a ferry angle is a matter of feel, and it requires practice. Too great an angle and you may lose control and be swept downstream; too small an angle and your sideways movement may be virtually undetectable. It's always best to be a little cautious at the start of any ferry; it's a lot easier to get the right angle than it is to recover it

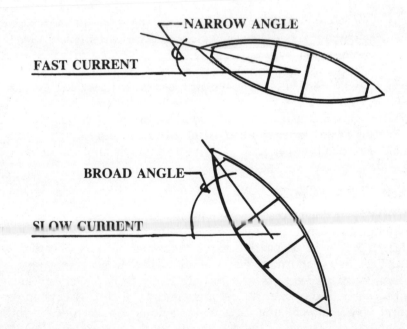

THE RELATIONSHIP OF FERRY ANGLE AND CURRENT SPEED

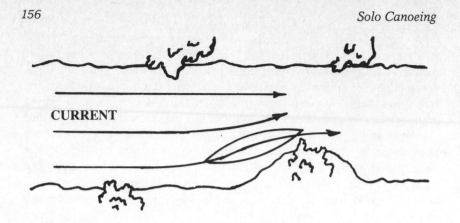

CURRENT

WHERE'S THE ANGLE?

when you've lost it by letting the canoe sweep down out of control! Assuming, however, you find an angle that works, you must control it as long as your ferry lasts.

The same strokes you used to set your angle will also control it: backstrokes and reverse sweeps for a back ferry; forward strokes and sweeps for a forward ferry, for example. You may also need to vary the ferry angle as the water conditions vary—the angle of the current changing, swifter water above a chute, or slower water below a ledge, for example. Watch where you're ferrying; be ready to adjust your angle. In approaching a stronger current, narrow your angle with the current just before you reach the stronger flow. In weaker currents you can adjust it any time.

Remember, you usually have a choice of speed versus work—a flatter angle and harder paddling, a sharper angle and easier paddling, or anywhere in between. Let the circumstances dictate your choice.

Back Ferry Mechanics

Halt your downstream movement if you can; slow it if you can't. Simultaneously angle the stern of your canoe in the direction you want to go: to your right to go to river right, to your left to move toward river left. The easiest and most effective strokes to do this are a reverse sweep or cross reverse sweep, as both apply back power and angle setting at the same time. Which you use first, of course, depends on which way you want to go and which side is your on side. In mild current the backstroke correction strokes work well, or you might use a backstroke and stern pry or backstroke and diagonal draw to the rear. There are many possibilities, so use whatever applies.

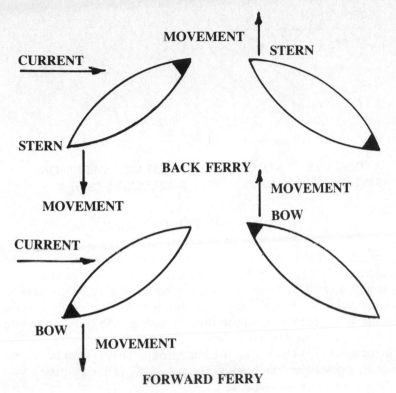

CURRENT

MOVEMENT

STERN

STERN

MOVEMENT

BACK FERRY

MOVEMENT

BOW

CURRENT

BOW

MOVEMENT

FORWARD FERRY

A CANOE FERRIES TO THE DIRECTION THE UPSTREAM
END IS POINTED

Do not use any forward strokes to set or control your angle and do not drag your paddle in the water behind you to turn the bow. Keep power on the boat and keep that power going in the right direction. This is a very common beginning mistake and a habit to absolutely avoid developing. Remember, your ferry is intended to *avoid* something downstream and the current is always trying to push you toward it. Don't help it by using the wrong strokes or doing nothing. Use your paddle effectively!

Forward Ferry Mechanics

Forward ferries are very easy to do in a solo canoe. Because of this you'll probably use them much more often than back ferries, particu-

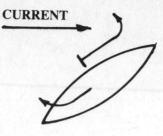

CURRENT

**CORRECTION STROKE   FORWARD SWEEP OR
OFTEN NECESSARY   FORWARD STROKE**

HOLDING THE FERRY ANGLE

larly for a long ferry or one across strong current. Doing a forward ferry instead of a back ferry has the advantage that you're facing in the direction you want to go so you can see better. Probably the biggest reason for using a forward ferry, however, is that it's a totally natural technique; all you are doing is paddling the canoe exactly as you would if you were paddling down the river.

To do a forward ferry, spin the boat around bow upstream. Keeping forward power on the boat, point your bow in the direction you want to go and set your angle. In a strong current it's easier to control the angle and keep your power going by using a forward stroke or forward sweep on the downstream side, so swap sides if you need or want to. In weaker currents you can usually control the angle and the power with your forward correction stroke.

From there the procedure is exactly as in a back ferry (except remember to do forward strokes). Adjust your angle for varying water conditions, do not use backstrokes or drag your paddle to turn the bow to correct your angle, and keep the forward power going. Should you lose your angle and end up bow downstream, just convert to a back ferry.

Practicing Ferries

Practice in slow-moving steady current. Experiment with your angle, slacking off on your paddle power more and more until you hit the right combination and literally feel the boat beginning to move across the current. If a more experienced paddler is along, get him or her to set your angle for you a few times until you know what you're looking for. Don't be in a hurry. Don't mistake paddling across the river for ferrying, and practice both forward and back ferries—you'll need both of them.

A final word on ferries: always remember you have two ferries to work with. If you're back ferrying, lose control of your angle, and the stern sweeps down, try to convert to a forward ferry. Similarly, shift to a back ferry if you find yourself completely out of position and bow downstream on an attempted forward ferry. In both cases, I'm assuming you have time and room enough to do this. In any event, anything beats laying your paddle across the gunwales and looking puzzled!

Other Maneuvers

Essing

Essing is a fun and useful maneuver. It's a combination peel off and eddy turn used to go from one eddy to another across a current. Although it's particularly useful if you feel the current is so strong it may overpower a ferry, you can use the technique anywhere you have the eddy-current-eddy situation. Essing can also compensate for the second eddy being farther downstream so you don't have to deliberately lose ground as you would with a ferry. It gives you an alternative in case you do try a ferry, lose your angle, and are swept downstream anyway, and it lets the river do even more of the work than does a ferry. Essing is so-called because of the S shape of the canoe's path when seen from above.

Essing is a very simple maneuver if you can do a peel off and eddy turn because it's simply a combination of the two done in one continuous technique. Start with a standard peel off, driving across the eddy line at an upstream angle, then leaning and bracing downstream as usual. Instead of letting the boat turn totally downstream, however, stop its turning at about a 45-degree downstream angle, and drive it into the far-side eddy. As you cross the eddy line, lean and brace into the turn as on any eddy turn.

Notice that whatever technique you use in the peel off, you will do the opposite technique in the eddy turn. For example, if you're paddling on the downstream side you would do an on-side peel off and an off-side eddy turn, in this case using a cross brace into the eddy. If you go back across and don't swap paddle sides, you would do an off-side peel off and an on-side brace back into the eddy where you started.

What you do to set up and control your entry angle into the far-side eddy depends upon the width and strength of the current you're crossing and whether you're paddling on the upstream or downstream

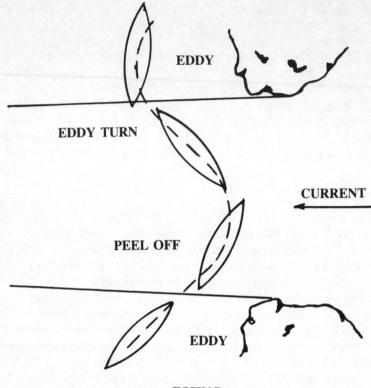

side. In general, it's always easier to start your peel off paddling on the downstream side. If you do, any of your steering strokes will control both your angle and power into the other eddy. For an off-side peel off, you might use some cross forward strokes to drive you on into the eddy, or for wider currents you may need to go back to your on-side for these power and control strokes.

Surfing

Surfing a solo canoe is another fun maneuver that also has very practical applications. You surf a canoe on a standing wave and can either just sit there in one place and enjoy the ride (this is the fun part) or use the maneuver to propel the canoe across the length of the wave with little or no effort. This is not only fun, but also a practical way to cross a current because you need to.

CURRENT

THE IDEA OF SURFING

In surfing a solo canoe, the boat faces upstream. Your bow is down in the trough of one wave and the stern up on the crest of the wave just downstream. You are literally sitting on a sloping wall of water, balanced between gravity trying to pull you down the hill into the upstream trough and the river trying to pull you back off the crest downstream. Obviously the balance point is critical, and it will take practice before you can find this point with any degree of precision. The angle

Side surfing. Good practice for braces, and fun too!

of the boat to the current is equally critical. To simply sit in one place, the hull has to be perfectly aligned with the current. Your job is to put in whatever paddle strokes are necessary to keep it in that position.

Crossing a current by surfing is done exactly like a forward ferry – angle the bow toward the desired direction and hold that angle. If done correctly, the canoe will be pulled across the crest of the wave in the direction of the bow. In this case you will probably need to put in some downstream paddle strokes (sweeps work very well) to both hold the angle and prevent the canoe from sliding off the wave toward downstream. If you hit everything just right, you'll often only have to lean and high brace downstream to be carried across.

Surfing done to cross a current doesn't always have to be in the bow-down position described. It can often be done in a more up or level position on the crest of the downstream wave. The balance point, however, is often a little trickier to hit. If you fall off into the upstream trough so you're sideways (broached), the river will try to roll you over upstream. Counter this with a strong downstream lean and brace. This side-surfing is often done for fun in souse holes. Use either high or low braces (or both) as required to keep you upright.

Powering up on a surfing wave is hard to do. Commonly you'll come in sideways from the end of the wave in a slight forward ferry angle, then align the boat as soon as you're in position if you want to "sit" on the wave. You'll hold your angle if you want to go on across. Another method is to go upstream of the wave and drift slowly back down on to it, putting in some strong forward strokes to stop your downstream movement when you're in position.

You can't surf on every standing wave in a river. Your weight, the weight of your canoe, the speed of the current and the configuration of the wave all enter into what makes a surfing wave. The point is, don't immediately decide you're doing it wrong if your surfing doesn't always work. You'll soon learn both how to handle the boat and how to select a wave.

Rolling the Open Canoe

It's easy to roll an open canoe – part way! It happens all the time on rivers. Rolling it back upright without coming out of the boat is trickier, but it's perfectly possible. Obviously, your hull must have a lot of flotation in it so only the cockpit area is flooded; it's little use to right a canoe that's full of water. You must also be able to stay in it upside down, so you need a saddle or thigh straps and foot braces. Finally, you need practice and, preferably, instruction. Practice in a pool or still water and have someone there to help you position your paddle

One Way to Roll the Solo Canoe

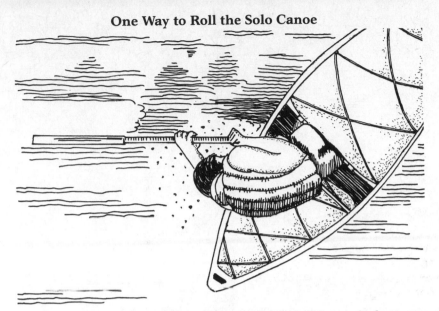

Sweep the paddle (power face down) from the bow to beside your body on your off side.

Pull down on the paddle and simultaneously rotate it so the nonpower face is down.

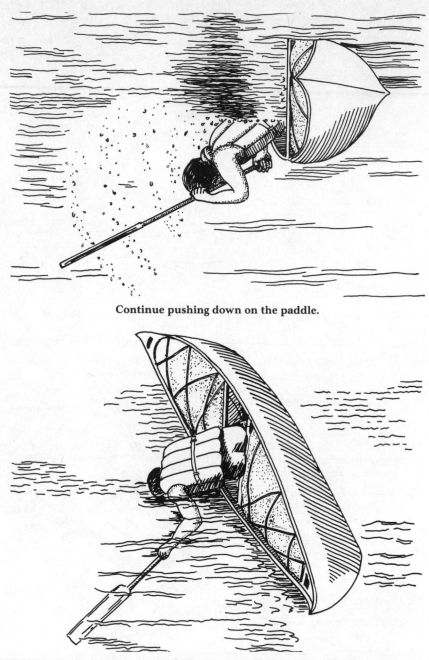

Continue pushing down on the paddle.

Snap your hips under you and lean to your paddling side. Continue pushing. You should now be coming up out of the water.

Push yourself completely upright.

All of the above motions must be done as one continuous action. Lean to the side, not forward, and bring your head out of the water last.

and help you roll up when you don't make it on your own. It's usually easier for most paddlers to roll up on one side than the other, but you should be able to roll either way with equal facility.

The drawings will give you an idea of one way this is done, maybe even enough of an idea to do it. Nose clips are a great idea during practice. So is a buddy to help you roll back up when you don't make it on your own.

8

Water Reading

Knowing how to maneuver a canoe is important, but it's only half the battle of river running. The other half is knowing *where* to maneuver, and that means knowing how to read water. Water reading consists of two things: recognizing a floatable, navigable path, and recognizing whatever obstacles may be in or near that path. Obviously the two are inseparable. Both require practice and experience. You'll be fooled many times before you learn the fundamentals and you'll still be fooled after you have some knowledge and experience, but not as often!

Water Behavior

Water in a river doesn't all flow along at the same speed; its velocity varies at different points in the riverbed. Generally the swiftest portion of any current is on or near the surface in the middle of the main flow. It is slowest near the bottom and the shoreline because of the friction between the water and the material of the riverbed. The closer the water is to the bed, the slower it flows.

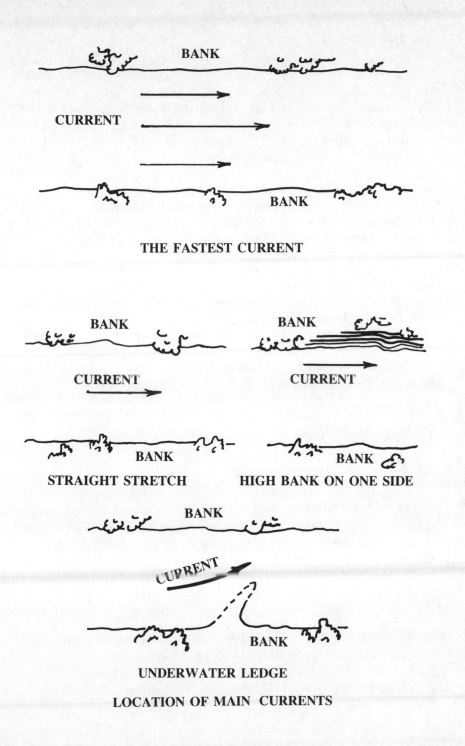

THE FASTEST CURRENT

STRAIGHT STRETCH

HIGH BANK ON ONE SIDE

UNDERWATER LEDGE

LOCATION OF MAIN CURRENTS

The Main Current

On a straight, unobstructed stretch of river, the main flow and thus the fastest current and deepest channel will be down the center of the river parallel to the banks. If one bank is higher than the other, the river is usually deepest and fastest near the higher bank. If an angled ledge occurs in the river, the main flow will probably be toward the downstream end of the ledge. Obstructions in the river will also divert the main current, but where it's diverted to is a question of the placement of the obstruction. It could be flowing in almost any direction and path and could also constantly change that direction and path.

In a smooth bend the main current and deepest water will be to the outside of the bend. In multiple smooth bends it will be from the outside of one bend, across the river, to the outside of the next bend. The inside curves of these bends will have eddies in them – slack water moving much slower than the main current, possibly not moving at all, or even flowing slightly upstream. These inside bends are likely to be shallow because the slower current of the eddy has deposited silt and pebbles to build up a bar.

Sharp bends, where the bend approaches or exceeds 90 degrees or more, present a different picture, and different problems. With much water volume or speed the current force on the *inside* of the bend will actually get stronger as the bend nears. As it strengthens, it will try to push you out and across the river into the opposite bank or into the confused current where the two flows of water meet. In addition, the inside may well be eddyless until you're actually around the bend.

Particulars about Outside Bends

If standing waves occur in a smooth bend, then they will be biggest on the outside of the bend because of the higher volume of water there. Similarly, because of this higher volume, the bank of an outside bend is quite likely to be undercut or eaten away, which can present the very real danger of fallen trees (strainers) in the water at these points.

Eddies

Eddy water is distinguishable from the rest of the river because it moves at a slower speed than the surrounding current, seems not to move at all, or even moves upstream in a circular manner. Eddies are your haven of safety and rest in the turbulent world of moving water. You can run into one and sit securely while the water rushes by on

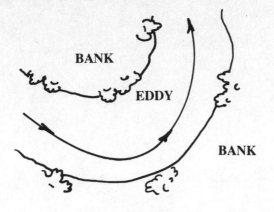

SINGLE BEND

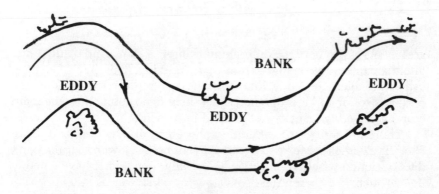

MULTIPLE BENDS

LOCATION OF MAIN CURRENT IN BENDS

either side of you. Eddies give you a place to rest, a place to plan your next move, or simply a place to sit and watch your fellow canoeists or the scenery.

Depending upon the current and the obstruction, the current differential between the main river and the water of the eddy will be

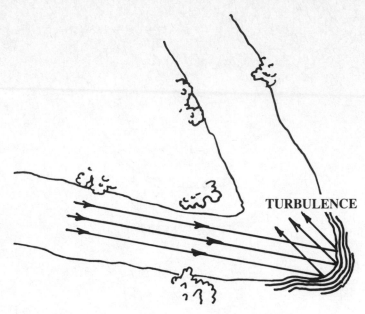

EXTREMELY SHARP BENDS

greater or less. Where the differential is large, a sharp and distinct line often separates the main current and the eddy. This line of demarcation is called the eddy line. With less differential this eddy line becomes softer and less distinct; often there is no actual line, the main current and eddy just gradually blend into each other.

There are three types of eddies: shoreline, obstruction, and bend. Shoreline eddies are formed by the current being slower near the bank due to friction with the shoreline. Generally they do not have an eddy line as such; the current just gets slower and slower as you approach the bank. They are generally the easiest eddies to enter and leave, although you may have to keep paddling a little (or hang on to a convenient bush or tree) to stay in them.

Bend eddies, as pointed out before, occur on the inside curve of turns in the river. They may or may not have a distinct eddy line and are usually easy to enter and exit, although you may need to use your peel-out and eddy-turn techniques to avoid flipping as you do. Usually a bend eddy is shallow (because a bar has been built up there) and often the bank of the inside curve is lower, making a good place to go ashore.

Obstruction eddies are formed by anything that breaks the current

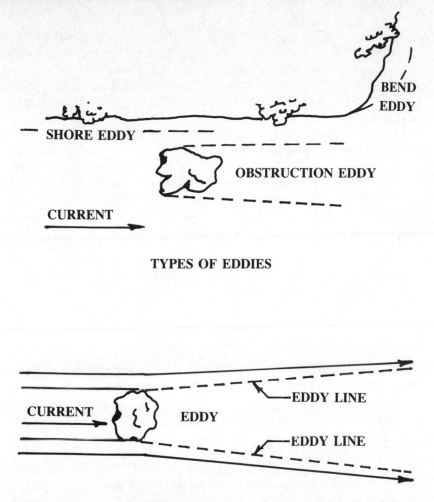

TYPES OF EDDIES

AN EDDY AND ITS EDDY LINE

enough to force the river to flow around it or slightly over it. This
can be an island, a log, a bridge pier, a protrusion from the shore, or,
most commonly, a rock. They generally have sharper, more distinct
eddy lines than either bend or shoreline eddies, but this depends
on the river flow and the configuration of the obstruction. Usually it's
best to enter and leave these eddies with your peel-out and eddy-turn
maneuvers.

Signs

Particular conditions in a river cause the water to act in particular ways. These are your signs, and once you learn to read them, they indicate to you what's happening in or under the water. Unfortunately, these signs are more often seen in combination than in their pure form, so, to the beginning canoeist, a rapid often presents an unfathomable picture of confusion.

The best way to unlock the confusion and to learn to pick out the various basic signs and conditions is to get an experienced river canoeist to point them out to you on the river itself. You can expand these fundamentals by your own study, observation, and testing. Once you do learn them, the apparently random flowing of the water won't be nearly as confusing.

One good way to learn is to scout a rapid – look at it from the top, the bottom, and from along the shore on the side. These different perspectives will help you spot the cause of many of the signs, as well as pick a path through the rapid. While you're scouting, look for the largest outflow of water and try to trace it back up the river – another good pathfinder. Practice will pay off. It won't be long before you find yourself beginning to distinguish the patterns of the water and automatically selecting a path.

Vs, Tongues, and Chutes

Vs are your first and most obvious guide to a floatable path. Formed by water being deflected around a rock (an upstream V) or being forced in between two rocks (a downstream V), they are unmistakable and easy signs, and often occur in combination. What is forming the V may not actually be showing above the surface, but the V reveals its presence. Obviously, you want to avoid the "point" of an upstream V; the downstream V, however, offers a first choice of path. It probably has been scoured out to a floatable depth, and it's also a clear path (at least for the duration of the V). Don't plunge blindly down Vs, however; look where they're taking you. It may be a place you don't want to go.

Tongues and chutes are sort of overgrown downstream Vs, and the three terms are often used interchangeably. Usually a tongue or chute is thought to have a more distinct elevation change between its up and downstream ends than a V and to have a higher volume and speed of water in it. Often they are formed by the water wearing down a softer section of rock in a ledge or ridge. They are also often found adjacent to large obstructions where the concentrated force of the water de-

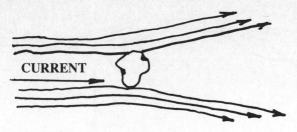

CURRENT

UPSTREAM

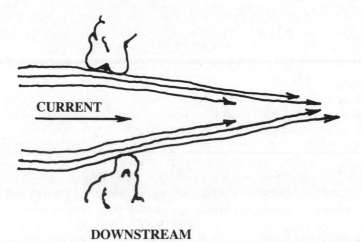

CURRENT

DOWNSTREAM

Vs

flected around the obstruction has scoured out a deeper channel. The end result is that the water pours down through a sort of slot as if it were running down a chute, hence the name. Tongues or chutes may be straight or curved but will have a relatively deep path to accommodate their higher volume and velocity.

Pillows and Waves

When water passes over a rock in a river, it creates various phenomena. Just what it creates depends on the shape and size of the rock, how far below the surface it is, and how much volume and speed the water has. In slow, deep water it usually does nothing and there is

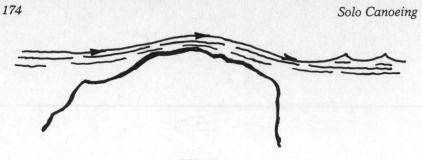

A PILLOW

no indication at all to guide you, even for a barely submerged rock; you either see it or you hit it! As the current increases, however, the water begins to form pillows. These are literally humps of water caused where rocks under the surface are so shaped that the water just flows smoothly over them instead of breaking over them. Pillows do form turbulence in the form of waves directly downstream of the rock. Even if you don't see the pillow, you can spot this turbulence.

As the current increases or the rock gets larger, these downstream waves increase in size and generally develop an upstream curl to their tops. If the current or volume is great enough or the shape of the rock is right, these waves may get so big this curl collapses on itself, forming what is often called a *roller* or *stopper* wave. Of course any good-size wave will slow you down if you dig your bow into it. Stopper waves, however, will often stop you dead in the water. With a boat full of flotation you won't swamp, but you are likely to broach and roll over if you don't have a strong, reliable downstream brace—and even then you may roll. You'll usually be swept on out, however, even if you do temporarily lose your boat.

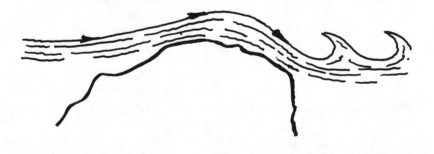

A CURLING WAVE

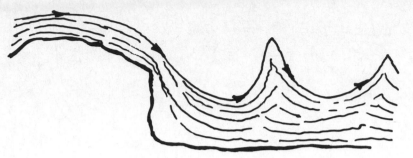

STANDING WAVES

Standing Waves

Standing waves, sometimes called *haystacks*, are very friendly waves – up to a point. They are caused by fast water suddenly hitting deeper, slower-moving water, so standing waves are usually a sign of a safe deep-water path. They are called standing waves because their wave form stands in the same place while the water moves through them, unlike ocean waves that move and break. Generally there is a string of standing waves, progressively smaller as you get farther away from the base of the chute, where they're usually found. Standing waves can be fun, like riding a roller coaster; all you need to watch for is the occasional rock you'll find in them, detectable by the curling wave below them or the shadow of the rock under the water. If the waves are too big, you may want to skirt along their edges. You'll wash right on through standing waves if you spill in them.

Souse Holes and Hydraulics

Although these two terms are often used interchangeably, I like to separate them with this distinction. One is potentially deadly and the other not.

Souse holes are the deep holes formed downstream of a rock when water pours over it. Depending on the size of the hole, you may nose into the upstream face of the wave, broach and sink if you haven't got enough flotation, roll if you haven't a strong enough brace, or you may plow on through the wave. As in standing waves, you'll be swept on out if you lose your boat. Hydraulics are another story altogether.

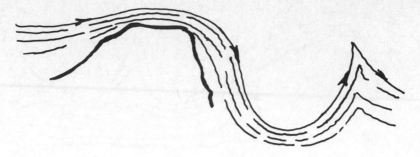

A SOUSE HOLE

Often called *keepers* when used in reference to souse holes, hydraulics can do exactly that – keep you and your canoe trapped in the circulating current of the hole.

Hydraulics are usually found at the base of waterfalls, dams, ledges, and slopes, where a large volume of water is pouring over the smooth lip of the obstruction, hitting the relatively still water below, and plunging toward the bottom. The descending water literally punches a hole in the water below and the surface water downstream is pulled into this hole. The result is a circulating current that is first pulled upstream then forced downward again by the descending water. This mass creates downward, reverse currents that can pull you under, roll and tumble you, push you up toward the surface, then pull you under again – all right at or near the base of the falling water. You can observe this action at the foot of any dam with a good flow of water over it. You'll often see fence posts, trees, or stumps vanishing in the froth beneath the falling water, then popping to the surface somewhere downstream and being pulled back upstream on the surface, only to be tumbled and sunk again. That post or stump could be you; the only difference is that the stump doesn't have to breathe!

Hydraulics are particularly likely to occur where solid sheets of water pour over a smooth slope or lip. Man-made obstructions such as dams are particularly prone to them, and even low dams can be extremely dangerous. Hydraulics are easy to spot. If you see standing waves running out below a drop, you know that even if you spill or swamp, you and your boat will be swept out downstream. If you do *not* see standing waves below it, however, look closely for an *upstream* current. An easy indication is bits of material drifting upstream on the surface, being pulled under, and reappearing downstream again to begin their upstream journey once more. This visible upstream current or lack of standing waves when there is a large volume of water pouring over something is a sure sign of a hydraulic—a whirlpool laid on its side, if you will, and one of the biggest dangers in canoeing.

Small hydraulics occur all over a river; almost any drop will have one. Often you can ride right through or over them and never know they're there. But when the river is high, the drop smooth, the volume great, or the conditions right, beware of them. Their danger under these conditions cannot be overemphasized. Hydraulics can be, and are, killers!

Drops, Falls, Ledges

In terms of water reading, these are all basically the same situation: vertical or nearly vertical descents over a short horizontal distance. At the foot of any of them you may find hydraulics whose size, depending on the water volume, height of the drop, and configuration of the obstruction, may be treated with caution or ignored.

Any flat, even-lipped drop is easy to spot from a canoe because the lip will form a sharp horizon line across the river, and the downstream scenery will be noticeably lower. Sharp slopes and the beginnings of rapids with a marked elevation drop will also often present this sharp horizon. You will also usually begin to see the whitewater or water vapor in the air at or above the line as you get closer.

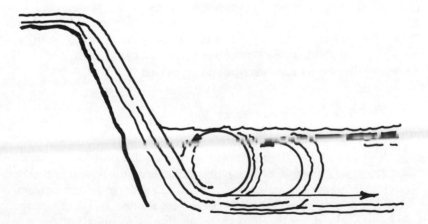

CURRENTS IN A HYDRAULIC

A series of ledges will be readily identified by the flat areas in between the drops and the froth and standing waves kicked up below them by the multiple (usually) chutes and Vs. Hydraulics and souse holes also are fond of lurking at the bottoms of falls and ledges, so be careful. Remember that in high, swift water you may not be able to back off if you approach too closely.

Slicks, Pebbled Surfaces, and Rock Gardens

Slicks and pebbled surfaces are indications of shallow water. A rock garden may or may not be shallow, but in the usual sense of the term it frequently is.

A slick is just what it sounds like: a very smooth, slick-looking patch in the midst of the general rough surface of the water. Slicks are caused by a smooth and flat-topped ledge or boulder very close to the surface. It's best to avoid them as they're often too shallow to float over.

Pebbled surfaces occur where the water is shallow and where the bottom is fairly even but has a lot of small obstructions of about the same height. Submerged gravel bars give a good example of this surface, as do sloping bars built up on the inside of bends in a river and at the outflow of streams and creeks entering a river.

A rock garden is a stretch of river with many rocks in it. While this could be called a rapid or a shoal, a rock garden is usually considered to be relatively shallow and have low-volume water that is so obstructed with rocks protruding above the surface it requires many maneuvers to negotiate its twists and turns. Rock gardens are good places to practice maneuvers and fun to work in if you're in no hurry. They are *not* fun when you encounter a really shallow one at the end of a long day on the river. It is at this stage of a trip that they're usually called more powerfully descriptive things than "rock gardens."

Miscellaneous Things to Watch For

Cushions

When water hits the upstream face of a solid obstruction, it often banks up in front of it before being deflected and flowing on downriver. This mass of piled-up water is called a cushion and can *sometimes* be used to hold you off or whip you around the obstruction. It may at least reduce the impact somewhat. Cushions are most frequently found and used where the water is banking off a rock whose face is sloping downstream and into or toward the main current. This

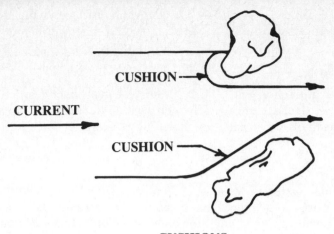

CUSHIONS

buffer will often effectively send you on around the rock and through the chute. A lack of a cushion on an obstruction in fast current could be a sign of a dangerous undercut; stay clear of it. In connection with this let me emphasize that water is *not* deflected by anything that it can pass through or easily pass over or under, such as most downed (undercut) trees and log jams. Safe cushions are formed only by solid, comparatively massive obstructions, and their use is a matter of their size and your experience.

Color

The color of the water in a river sometimes offers a clue to what's in it (or not in it). In calm water a darker color can almost be relied upon to mean deeper water and a lighter tone to mean shallower water. In rapids, although slicks and hard-to-detect pillows can also create dark spots, a darker tone will usually still indicate a possible path, although it could also indicate a submerged rock. You'll have to watch the general colors in the particular river you're in to become aware of just what changes mean what. Of course, color means little in a muddy river.

Terrain

The shoreline can offer you some clues to approaching water conditions. If the banks start to get higher and earth banks begin to give way to rock formations and cliffs, you can almost rely on a shoal or a rapid coming up or at least a deeper, swifter, narrower channel.

Speed of Water

In conjunction with the last item you'll probably notice that as cliffs rise, river speed generally increases. In flat areas a drop in elevation ahead of you is usually signaled by accelerated current.

Frothy Water

Frothy water is water so full of air from being tossed up and churned around in a rapid that it can barely be treated as water. While it is not really a sign of anything except a lot of turbulence, you should be aware of its properties before you read the water, find a path, and paddle headlong into this unwaterlike froth.

Basically, frothy water is so thin and offers such little resistance, support, and body that your canoe will drop in farther than you expected it to, paddle strokes and braces may not be effective, and should you spill, your life jacket won't support you as you think it should. The degree to which this happens depends upon how much white is in this path of whitewater. The more active the rapid and the higher the water is tossed, the more frothy it becomes and the more you can expect these effects. Go ahead and paddle into it, but realize that it won't support you like a solid mass of water.

One More Sign

On any river your ears will usually tell you of an approaching shoal or rapid before your eyes do. This comes in very handy at any time but particularly so when rounding bends on strange rivers or when you're paddling in poor viewing conditions such as the late evening, dark, rainy days, or facing into a late afternoon sun glinting off the water. Of course, just hearing something doesn't tell you much because any obstructed water or small drop makes a noise out of all proportion to its size and ferocity.

Reading "Impossible" Water

Early in your water-reading and canoeing career you will probably run across a lot of rapids that you will find impossible to read. Either there is no apparent path or none that you think you can follow, or there are drops that you're not willing to run, heavier volume and stronger current that you're used to, potential stoppers, or any number of things that make this particular rapid more than you're willing to try. As your experience and skill increase you will find that your rating of rapids decreases and that many of these impossible, no-path jumbles of water, froth, and rock are possible and do have paths. But, for your own safety, be cautious. Don't overmatch yourself! There are only two situations in which you should try to run a rapid that's impossible for you. One is as part of a training program where qualified instructors are there to help you, and the other is when other experienced canoeists are along to help you. In both cases the run should be made with rescue canoes and people with throwing ropes stationed along the way (at least at the bottom of the rapid). If you're alone (and you shouldn't be) or if all in your group (no matter how experienced) find the rapid impossible, portage it. There is nothing cowardly or disgraceful about this; it just makes very good sense. It's your canoe, your equipment, and your life, and it's stupid to risk them because of what you think someone else may think.

9

Safety and Rescue

Safety is not a universally popular subject. To some people the very word means a depreciation of enjoyment, a hindrance, and a threat to their egos. Yet most experienced canoeists, consciously or unconsciously, generally follow the basic canoeing safety rules; most of them learned that rules are nothing more than an extension of common sense based on specific knowledge of the hazards of canoe trips, and have an innate desire to preserve equipment and to remain alive and in one piece.

In the beginning you may consider some of the tactics of more experienced canoeists as totally foolhardly, but often what you are witnessing is a product of knowledge, experience, practice, and technical ability, and not a desire to just show off or take unnecessary risks. In brief, the ardent practice of safety and the exercise of appropriate caution is not a sign of weakness, only of good sense and a desire to continue canoeing to a ripe old age!

Rivers and Lakes – The Big Difference

Even a shallow river with a moderate flow is strong and heavy, a fact not appreciated by many beginning river canoeists until they find their canoe pinned solidly against some river rock and discover they can't get the hull loose without a lot of help. The situation effectively demonstrates the important point of difference between paddling the waters of a lake and the waters of a river – the presence of a current.

River canoeists learn to use this current as an actual aid in maneuvering. In the process they absorb some fundamental behavior rules for moving water that allow them to offset some of the force or to otherwise use it to their advantage. Obviously, lake-trained canoeists don't need such knowledge or techniques; they rarely encounter any current and, disregarding wind, have only the controllable power of their paddle strokes acting on the hull.

The point is that still-water techniques can swiftly get you into trouble on moving water. And the specialized river techniques – many of which can't even be learned or practiced in still water – are essential in moving water. You do need to have some basic still-water canoeing skills, but if you're going to canoe on rivers, you also need the specialized river-canoeing skills. It's something like learning to drive a car. Learn on a straight shift, and you can easily drive an automatic, but it doesn't work the other way. Similarly, river-canoeing techniques are much more adaptable to lakes than are lake techniques to rivers.

These river or moving-water techniques are essential from a safety standpoint. They need to be taught to you and practiced when there is no penalty for the errors we all make, which means in the company of experienced canoeists. Trial and error on the river, especially alone, can cost you a canoe and possibly a life.

River and Paddler Ratings

Through the years as river canoeists bounced and splashed their way down various streams (or tried to), it became obvious that dangerous mismatches of river and paddler were likely to occur. Some uniform way to describe the difficulty of the water and the degree of expertise of the canoeist and to relate these two factors together was not only necessary, but rather vital. The results of this demand were some guidelines attempting to do just that. Obviously such guides must be somewhat general; equally obviously, individual opinion must play a big part in determining both river difficulty and paddler proficiency. The guides, however, do present the best available method of arriving at a relatively accurate representation of the all-important combination of paddler and river. You'll find these charts in the appendix. Get familiar with all of them, as they're all still in use.

General Safety

Mishaps on a river can occur for many reasons. Some are created by basic inexperience and lack of canoeing knowledge. Others result from a lack of planning, such as too long a trip for the time you have. Still others are caused by unpredictable things such as bee stings, snakebite, and sudden storms. The list of what could happen is endless. Fortunately, serious mishaps are relatively few, considering the number of canoes on today's rivers. However, you should be aware of possible mishaps, and know how to avoid or lessen them with the elementary precautions of basic safety.

One *very* basic rule is to follow the safety code in the appendix of this book. It was developed over a period of time by experts in the canoeing field from their own experiences and those of thousands of other canoeists. This code should become habit with you, and you should try to impress other canoeists with its value too. Listed here are a few of the other aspects of river safety that should also become automatic with you.

Before You Leave

Get Some Facts

Every river and section of river will be new to you the first time you run it. The best and safest way is always to make your first trip on it with someone who has run it before. If this isn't possible, take these precautions. First off, gather what background information is available and examine the section of the river you're going to run from all the access points you can. Don't overrate your ability, and don't go alone. Strictly observe all the recommended safety precautions and rules (see the appendix). Ease around the inside of bends, and keep looking as far ahead as you can until you're around them. Check the river ahead and on the sides for sharp lines that might indicate a drop, and listen for the noises of shoals and rapids ahead. Finally, don't run a river when it's flooded. In the winter be particularly aware of cold-water hazards and cautious of high, swift water, and be doubly safety conscious.

Let Someone Know of Your Trip

Don't just hop in a river and take off. Let someone know when and where you're going. Include in this information your put-in, your take-out, and your estimated time of arrival at the take-out. This way if you do get in trouble, at least everybody knows when to start worrying, and, if you haven't had a last-minute change of plans, the searchers know the general area in which to start looking.

On The Trip

Allow Enough Time

Allow enough time for travel to the put-in and for shuttling, plus enough (and a little more) for the trip. Start early; don't get caught out on the river with darkness closing in. If you do get caught by darkness, don't try to pick your way down the river by guess, flashlight, listening, or luck; just pull to the shore before dark and take off for the nearest road if there's one close enough. If not, settle down for the night. Here's where a map of the area would come in handy.

Be Prepared for a Few Emergencies

Carry along a throw rope and a basic personal first aid kit. Learn the fundamental first aid measures for such things as shock, severe cuts, and heat-related conditions. Waterproof matches may be handy any time and are vital in cold weather. In winter have an extra set of clothes, something that will quickly start a fire, and a knowledge of hypothermia and frostbite.

Paddling Alone

Don't! At least not if "alone" means just you and your canoe. The recommended minimum number on a trip is two canoes or three people. While there is nothing wrong with lone canoe trips under certain circumstances, each trip should be considered in the light of river conditions and your experience. Just be sure your knowledge and experience are enough to qualify you to correctly evaluate the circumstances and risks and your paddling proficiency is sufficient for them. Don't ignore the nonpaddling mishaps that could also happen; they may happen only once in a lifetime to you, but how do you predict when that once may be?

Of course, there are times when it's just tempting fate to go alone and it shouldn't be done at all. Don't go off down any unknown river alone unless you know from a good guidebook what to expect or know someone who is familiar with that stretch, and your information tells you it's peaceful and easy. Don't go alone down any river with anything on it greater than a Class I rapid, and don't do it then unless you're an experienced river canoeist and are thoroughly familiar with that stretch. Even then it's not a good idea. Don't go alone down any river in cold weather, when the river is high or flooded (of course, all canoeists should stay off flooded rivers anyway), or on any narrow, swift rivers.

Too cautious? Maybe so, but years of paddling and teaching have taught me that mishaps happen when least expected. So don't canoe alone until you know enough *not* to canoe alone. When you reach that stage you're ready to try it occasionally.

Flooded Rivers

Stay off them. Not only does high water completely change the face of an otherwise familiar river, but it sweeps along tree limbs, tree trunks, whole trees, and all sorts of other things that can smash or entangle your canoe and you. High water undercuts shoreline trees and creates hazards on the outside of bends in the form of standing waves and trees partially toppled in the river. Islands disappear, leaving only the tops of trees stuck out of the water to possibly catch you. The shoreline may be under water and, in some rivers, you may actually lose the river and find yourself swept into trees and bushes with no idea of which way to go to the main riverbed. On the top of this is the sheer weight, speed, and power of fast-moving, high-volume water. The power can overcome your efforts to combat it as if you were doing nothing, and the speed dramatically reduces your available decision and reaction time.

Of course, there's always the question of whether the river actually is flooded! Often it's obvious, but at those iffy levels, it's a question of your experience and knowledge of that particular run at other levels.

Strainers

Log jams, tree limbs in the water, small openings between boulders are all perfect examples of places water can flow through but your canoe can't. They're called strainers because that's what they do — stop or "strain" you and your boat out of the water. The pressure of the flowing water can then plaster you and your canoe up against whatever is forming the strainer, and it doesn't take much pressure to hold you there for good. Strainers are *very* dangerous.

Overconfidence

This is the downfall of many canoeists. Canoeing looks so simple and easy when someone knowledgeable is paddling along, but then so do ski jumping, surfing, and handling rattlesnakes. Probably the worst thing that can happen to a brand-new, totally unskilled canoeist is to actually luck his way down through some rough rapids the first time out. The bad part is that he usually begins to think he's invincible and continues on in this foolhardy manner, until one day when his luck deserts him and only the skills that he never bothered to learn can save him. Not that I want any canoeist hurt or his canoe destroyed, but a good scare, a few bad bends of canoe parts, and a small hole or two in the hull go a long way toward demolishing the idea of super-paddler!

Natural Hazards

Mama Nature may or may not like canoeists, but she's put some natural hazards out there on and around her rivers that you should remember. Hornets, bees, and wasps are three, usually not fatal except to those with a particular allergy to their sting. Snakes of the poisonous variety are another, and usually one or more of the four types the United States is blessed with are found somewhere all around our country. Snakebite is rather uncommon, but, as canoeists and snakes tend to be out more in the warmer months, reasonable caution should be used. Poison ivy and oak make a lot of people wish they had resisted the itch to get outdoors. And, of course, there's always heat and cold taking their toll. Lightning travels well in water and likes to strike tall sheltering trees along the shore too.

Some of these natural hazards can be treated with the contents of a simple first aid kit. Others can be avoided by common sense, caution, and, very important, some advance knowledge of their likelihood and treatment.

Cold-Weather Canoeing

Winter canoeing presents its own hazards. There are fewer canoeists out; ergo: less available help. Rivers are usually higher and swifter, the air and water colder, and inclement weather more likely. All the precautions of summer apply, plus a few more.

Some Rules for Winter

Never boat alone in cold weather, and be sure your canoeing partners know what hypothermia is, what the symptoms are, and what to do about it. Dress for the expected weather, but don't discount unexpected weather. Wind and wetness are more to be guarded against than cold, so take your rainsuit and wear or take a windproof shell over your clothing. Wear a wet suit if the temperature calls for it, or if you're particularly susceptible to cold. Wear a hat and gloves with whatever clothing you have on.

Carry waterproof matches and something to start a fire with. A pint or even a half-pint container of camp-stove fuel or kerosene will help get a fire going in a hurry. Don't rely on nonwaterproof matches even in a watertight container. A short exposure to rain, the humidity of a raw day, or trying to strike them on a wet surface can cause them to crumble. Put a striker in your match case, under the cap for example, then load waterproof matches in the case with heads away from the striker.

Always carry a complete change of clothes in something waterproof, and a pocket or sheath knife. If your waterproof container is tied in (as it should be), you may not be able to untie it if your hands are cold or the knots are frozen. With a knife you can cut them loose. It's a good idea to carry a towel too. Just drying your body off will help your comfort a lot. You might also consider carrying another complete change of clothes to leave in your vehicle; you could go in twice.

Spills and Chills

Immersion in cold water because of spills, wading out to rescue a boat, or whatever reason, tremendously increases body heat loss. The cold water saps your strength rapidly, and you immediately get the sensation of numb hands and feet and soon begin to lose control of your limbs and hands. This makes it harder or impossible to do anything useful for you or anyone else. Your trunk is swiftly robbed of its warmth, and hypothermia begins to set in. When this happens you are not only incapable of helping yourself but also of even knowing that you need help. You may drown or you may die of hypothermia. One is as fatal as the other.

All this is not instantaneous, of course, but it does point out the necessity of getting out of cold water or a cold situation as rapidly as possible. Depending upon the water temperature and your susceptibility to cold, you have a varying amount of time. After you get out of the water you are doubly prone to chill factor and may be on your way into hypothermia, but you're still better off than you were in the water. As an example, the average person usually has less than thirty minutes to total helplessness in 40-degree water unless wearing a wet suit.

Hypothermia

Hypothermia is a condition in which your normal temperature begins to drop and your body cannot halt the process. The body loses heat faster than it can produce it, and in so doing uses up its energy reserves. When this reserve is exhausted, hypothermia begins; the

CORE TEMPERATURE	SYMPTOMS
99°–96°	Shivering, slurred speech, loss of reasoning
96°–86°	Stumbling, weakness, loss of control of hands, confusion
86°–80°	Sleepiness, inability to walk, collapse
80°–78°	Unconsciousness
78°–Down	Death

This chart is an average. Individuals are likely to vary widely in their susceptibility to low temperatures.

AVERAGE HYPOTHERMIA REACTIONS

WATER TEMPERATURE	"SAFE" TIME (MINUTES)	POSSIBLE SURVIVAL TIME (HOURS)
30°	20	1½
40°	30	2
50°	60	3¾

AVERAGE APPROXIMATE TIME TO HELPLESSNESS IN COLD WATER
(Non-wet suit, in conventional winter clothing.)

core temperature continues down until you lose consciousness, go into a coma, and die. Hypothermia is a direct result of exposure to wind, wet, and cold, and is one of the biggest hazards of winter canoeing. Its two great dangers: more cases of hypothermia occur in the relatively warm temperature between 30 and 50 degrees when you don't expect it than they do in really cold weather, and by the time you are in the first stages of hypothermia, you are too far gone to realize it. Just the threat of hypothermia should convince you not to canoe alone in the winter. You are helpless once it strikes you, and your only hope is to forestall it by being aware of it and trying to keep out of situations likely to incur it.

Aid for victims of hypothermia consists of furnishing heat to the body. Recommended treatment is first to remove the victim from the hypothermia-inducing environment. Get him out of the wind and rain and inside if possible, in a tent, cabin, or whatever is handy. Build a fire, remove his clothes if they are wet, and get him into dry clothes and something with good insulation such as blankets or a sleeping bag. Give him warm drinks and possibly apply warmed canteens, towels, and the like to his body.

If the victim is nearly unconscious, try to keep him awake and give him warm drinks. Don't strangle him by forcing warm drinks down him, but do try to get him to drink them. Leave him naked and put him into a sleeping bag or blankets with another naked person. If you can, sandwich him between two naked people. This may sound strange, but the skin-to-skin contact is a most effective treatment. If your victim is anywhere near this last stage of unconsciousness, you should try to get medical help if it's within reach. In the meantime, however, pursue the aid outlined above as far as possible. It could mean the difference between life and death. Don't give up on your efforts; there have been some miraculous recoveries by apparently dead victims of hypothermia.

Frostbite

Frostbite is indicated by a numb sensation and by a grayish white appearance of the affected part, usually fingers, toes, nose, ears, or cheeks. If not caught soon enough it can mean freezing and permanent damage or loss of the frostbitten part. Treatment is to thaw the frozen part, but not by rubbing with snow or anything else. Rubbing will do more damage than good. Warm the part by covering it with an un-gloved hand or, if it's a hand that is frostbitten, by putting it under your armpit after removing the glove. Get inside or at least out of the wind, and drink something warm. If the part is wet, dry it. If the skin doesn't respond to the hand warming, hold the part in likewarm water, if possible, or wrap it in something like warmed blankets or towels.

Some Ways to Help Keep Warm

Clothes of wool or, better yet, a wet suit – both complete with gloves, head covering, and foot covering – serve for insulation in the winter. Reduce chill-factor effect by covering the wet suit or clothes with a windproof jumpsuit or at least a paddling jacket. A lot of canoeists put on their rainsuit tops or the whole rainsuit in cold, windy weather, preferring the condensation inside to the wind chill outside.

Eat often, don't get hungry. Your body's heat factory needs fuel and that means food, so nibble along all day. When you stop to eat, take the time to fix something hot to eat or drink and to build a fire. Get out of the wind, rain, snow, or whatever the weather is.

Don't overtire yourself. Tiredness means you've used up your energy, and that means your body is low on the ability to produce heat. Stop early, don't push on to exhaustion.

Rescue

Rescues on a river fall into two big groups: the rescue of people and the rescue of boats. Of these, the rescue of people is far more important and, itself, has the two headings of self-rescue and rescue by others.

The Rescue of People

Two basic rules apply, whether you're engaged in self-rescue or helping someone else. The first is, save the people first. Worry about boats and equipment later. All or most of it will be recovered later anyway and, even if it's not, the paddlers are still more important. The second rule is, if you or your companions even *think* you're likely to spill in a rapid, wear your PFDs. They make rescue of anyone in the water easier and add tremendously to the safety factor for the victim.

Self Rescue

Rescue Yourself if Possible

Do not rely on others to rescue you. What assistance they give will be welcome and helpful, but do all you can to rescue yourself first.

Get into Swimming Position

Don't try to stand up in swift current! It's an instinctive thing to do, and it's instinctive to grab your canoe and try to hold it. Your instincts are wrong. You could too easily get a foot caught in something underwater, be knocked down by the current and drown, or, at best, be helpless. Instead get into swimming position immediately.

Position your body for maximum safety. Lie on your back, facing downstream, get your legs and feet together and in front of you, and keep both legs and body up as near the surface of the water as possible. Keep your knees bent and paddle with your hands to maintain this position. In this way you can see where you're going, exercise some control over your course, and both use your body as some protection yet guard it as much as possible from injury. Your legs act as bumpers and the bent knees as shock absorbers if you slam into something. Keeping body and feet near the surface prevents the tumbling and subsequent loss of control and leg cushion that could occur if you let your feet dangle into the slower-moving water below the surface.

Next, locate the canoe and make sure you're clear of it. This means

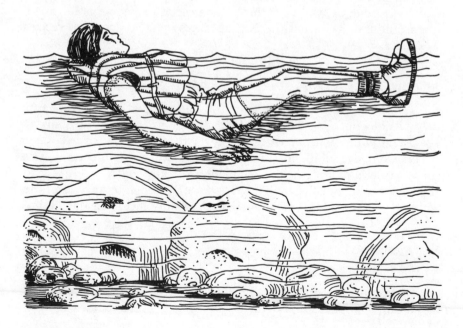

getting upstream of it. You don't want to be caught between it and some immovable object such as a rock. Even a moving empty canoe can hurt if it hits you; if it's swamped, it could easily crush you or inextricably pin you against something. Getting upstream of a canoe in moving water isn't as easy as it sounds. Things are happening fast and both you and the boat are being swept along at about the same speed. You may need to "handwalk" up the boat, pulling yourself along by holding the gunwales or whatever part you can grab. If everything happens too fast and you see (or know) you're being swept into a dangerous position, then abandon the boat and get clear of it, upstream preferably, but at least where it can't swing around and pin you.

Use the Canoe, or Abandon It

You may want to use your canoe as a safety device once you're in swimming position and in a safe location in regard to the boat, and have a second or so to assess the situation. It will provide a lot of flotation and can serve as a shield between you and whatever may be in the water. Stay in swimming position, hang on to the upstream end and on the upstream side of the boat, if the hull isn't aligned with the current. You might also hang on to the painter if it's available, but never loop the painter around your hand – the pressure could pull it so tight you can't get free. Be ready to swap sides; the boat could swing around and your safe upstream side suddenly become the unsafe downstream side.

Sometimes the best course is to abandon the boat and get yourself to safety. So, if hanging on to it is going to pull you into any situation that looks worse than the one you're in, *and you can improve your chances by doing so,* don't hesitate to abandon the boat and strike out on your own.

If the water and air are very cold, forget the canoe (unless that's the fastest and safest way to shore), and get yourself to shore or out of the water as soon as possible. Cold water will sap your strength quickly, and you don't need to waste what you have struggling with the boat.

Find an Eddy, a Rock, or Go To Shore

If no one is around to fish you out of the water, work your way to the shoreline or into an eddy by angling into the current and back-stroking; you'll go on downstream but at the same time slowly back

ferry your way to the shore or eddy. The eddy will at least get you out
of the current where you can rest and think and, if you still have it,
possibly empty your canoe and paddle to safety.

One consideration: if the water is very cold, there's no one on
shore to help you, and you can't climb out of the water on what is
creating the eddy, or you know you'll have to go right back in to reach
the shore, then use the eddy only briefly. Don't float there until you
succumb to hypothermia.

Swimming

Don't try to swim to safety in a strong current or a rapid. The river
is probably much stronger than you, and you'll only exhaust yourself.
Stay in your safe floating position until the water is clear of obstruc-

tions and the current is slow. I have seen some people successfully swim to safety, but it was a short distance, inspired by pure desperation and aided by luck!

Hydraulics

There is no guaranteed method of self-rescue from a hydraulic. The tumbling and the resultant confusion about up and down may aggravate your situation. Suggestions are to try to work out the *end* of the circulating current or to try to swim downstream along the bottom when it sucks you down. If you see standing waves and can get to them, they'll sweep you out to safety. Remember, hydraulics will bring you to the surface, thus offering you a chance to get a breath. Hydraulics are a very good reason to not boat alone and to have a rescue line along.

Don't Be Rule Bound

You're not in a great position to do too much when drifting in your life jacket in the water. Your field of view is limited, you may be being tossed around and up and down, and everything usually is happening fast. Be flexible. Adjust your actions to the circumstances. If the day is warm and you're in no danger, then grab the upstream end of the boat and enjoy the ride. If the situation is different, then do something different. Let the temperature of air and water, the presence or absence of companions, the turbulence of the river, the amount and proximity of obstructions, and, of course, the amount of time you have, determine what you do.

The Rescue of Others

Always set up rescue ropes at the site of likely spills — or even at unlikely ones, as they do happen now and again. Station rescue canoes at the bottom of the rapid, too, and make sure all paddlers wear their PFDs. With these precautions, the rescue of others is normally pretty straightforward, as you've already covered the two main ways: the use of ropes and the use of canoes.

Use a Canoe

This is the safest, easiest way of getting people to safety once they've cleared the rapid. Paddle out, have them hang on to your canoe or the painter, and tow them to safety. If you have room in your canoe (which most solo canoes do *not*), do a paddle brace and lean and get them in the boat. If their canoe is handy, empty it using the canoe-over-canoe method or whatever is easiest, and help them back in it. The canoe-over-canoe method is tricky in a solo boat, but can be done. How to is explained in the appendix.

Use a Throw Rope or Bag

The use of these ropes in rescue is more common than the use of a canoe; a well-thrown rope will bring the floater to safety with no danger to the rescuer. The effective use of a throw rope or bag takes some practice, and the art of throwing one has a few knacks about it that need some study. Again, the how-to of this very important subject is explained in the appendix. It does need practice, so practice before you really need it.

Wading and Swimming

This is absolutely not recommended as a rescue method. The chances are you will only end up with someone else to rescue. It has been done, and undoubtedly will be tried again, but it's very danger-ous. Exhaust all other possibilities first.

Hydraulics

If someone is caught in a hydraulic, rely on your throw rope to get him out. One good way to get the rope to him is to tie a PFD to the end of the rope and float it into the hydraulic. If the victim is unconscious or beyond helping himself and you must go in after him, go in *only* with a rope around your waist and someone handling the shore end. Never, even as a last resort, tie the rope to the shore. There is too great a likelihood that there will then be two of you caught in the hydraulic.

The Rescue of Canoes

The rescue of solo canoes is usually pretty simple. Commonly the boats are stuffed with flotation, which reduces their water weight when swamped. As they are also riding higher, they are not as likely to be caught and wrapped around a rock. In most situations, the problem is more getting to the boat and freeing it safely then actually getting it loose.

Emptying a Swamped Canoe

Any swamped canoe (or empty one, for that matter) is easier to handle when it's aligned with the current. Hang on to one end and let the current sweep the other end downstream. If you can work it into an eddy or to the shore, do so. If not, find a shallow place or rock to stand on (preferably in an eddy) and dump out the water by lifting the boat from one end or rolling it over. You can also drag one end up on a rock or the shore, letting the water run out the other end, or use the canoe-over-canoe rescue method described in the appendix.

Reentering a Canoe from the Water

Easier said than done in a slalom boat, although an agile person can do it. It's much simpler to climb in off a rock or have a paddler in another canoe steady yours while you're reentering. For the agile, however, the key is not to load all your weight on one gunwale and try to lift your body up, but to let the river support as much of your weight as it will for as long as it will. Position yourself at the widest point of the canoe where you can reach across to the opposite gunwale, put the other hand on the near gunwale, kick your feet up to the surface and sort of roll and kick your way in as you keep downward pressure on the opposite gunwale. Not graceful, and not easy either. Practice this before you need it.

Pinned and Hung Canoes

A hung canoe is just caught by an obstruction, as where you've ridden up on a shoal or rock. The upstream gunwale hasn't gone under and the boat is usually held only by weight and friction. A pinned canoe is more often pressed tight against an obstruction by water pouring in or over it. It may be totally or partially full of water and may even be bent around the obstruction by the force of the water. It's often *very* firmly held.

Exiting from a Hung or Pinned Canoe

The cardinal rule (almost) of exiting from a hung or pinned canoe in current is to get out *upstream* of the canoe. A hung boat may often be freed by simply taking some weight off of it. Sometimes that is just a matter of sticking one foot out and pressing down on the rock that's caught you. Sometimes, it's step all the way out. Regardless, step out upstream of the canoe. If the boat suddenly comes loose it could run over or pin you, neither of which is fun when the canoe is empty and could be highly dangerous or deadly if it's swamped. This could be the same situation as a "bear trap" where you are pinned between your canoe and an immovable obstruction.

Obviously there will be situations where you won't get out upstream, deep water upstream and a protruding rock downstream, for example. Nonetheless, as a general rule, do try to get out upstream. The idea is to locate yourself so you're in a safe position when the canoe comes free and is once more being pushed by the current.

Hang on to the Canoe

Before you step out of a hung canoe, put your paddle in the bottom of the canoe; never just lay it across the gunwales. Then, when you do step out, maintain a firm grip on the canoe in case it suddenly comes free and decides to go on its way without you.

Don't Let Hung Become Pinned

It's very easy for a hung canoe to become pinned. If you broadside on something, the upstream gunwale may immediately begin to sink. Swift action such as a hard lean downstream, leaping out onto an exposed rock downstream and pulling the canoe up on it, even (cautiously) jumping in upstream and lifting the gunwale may save the day. The idea is to stop the water pouring in the boat and making a bad situation worse.

Pinned Canoes

A pinned canoe is usually totally or partially swamped with the weight of the water in it and the force of the current against it holding it firmly against the obstruction. Fortunately, solo boats usually have lots of flotation so the problem is often not as severe as it could be. But, with or without flotation, a pinned boat can present real rescue problems. Unfortunately, there are no cut-and-dried methods. Each case has to be worked individually. There are a few helpful hints, however, that apply in all the cases.

First off, analyze the situation. If possible you want to make the water work for you; at worst you want to have it work against you as little as possible. Look at the position of the canoe and try to determine where the water is exerting the least pressure or where you can get the

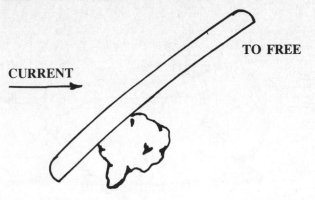

most leverage. If one end is stuck out in the current more than the other, work with this free end as the current will already be pushing at it and trying to dislodge it. All the pressure that is holding the canoe to the rock is up on a comparatively short section of the canoe. In this case you could use the current's help on the downstream end and try to work the canoe off in this direction by pulling on the caught end and gradually pivoting it around the rock or by lifting it as you pivot to reduce or stop the flow of water into the open top. The more you move it, the more the current on the downstream end will help you. Obviously, your first attempt would be to simply lift the short (upstream) end out of the water. If you succeed, the boat is free anyway.

With no free end but a slope in one direction, work in the direction of the slope. If one end is deep in the water and the other end clear, try working with the clear end if it's not going to get the underwater part in a worse bind. Other tricks to try include rolling the boat up out of

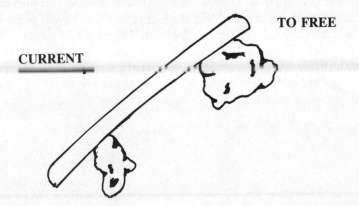

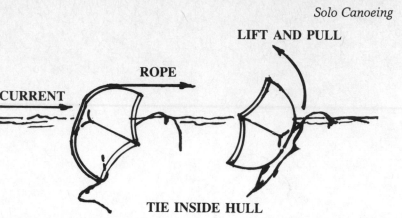

the water or lifting and rolling it. Depending on the situation, it may be easier (or better) to roll the upstream gunwale up and over toward downstream or the downstream gunwale up and over toward upstream. Tying a rope around the boat and heaving on it to roll the hull may be efficient. Use what manpower and ropes you have.

Get as many people out on the canoe as have room to work from a safe position. If the current is swift, use safety lines. Everyone should have on life jackets. Aid the efforts of those in the water with lines from shore or nearby firm footing and put more manpower on them. Don't tie directly to a thwart or seat; the chances are that they'll just bend, break, or rip out. Tie your hauling lines around the hull using a bowline or a slip knot. These ropes can be used to assist in the general effort to snub or hold what gains have been made, and sometimes to do all the work. Obviously, all efforts should be coordinated so that the rescuers are not working against themselves.

In general, the goal is to relieve the water weight and pressure on the hull. The more this is done, the easier the canoe will come loose. The first moves are the hardest. Try to find the path of least resistance to your pull and one that will do the most good. The basic rule is to try to work the canoe into a position ever more parallel with the current and to get the upstream gunwale up out of the water. Once either of these goals is met, your canoe is usually freed.

Appendix

The following pages contain a variety of general information of use to the solo canoeist, or any canoeist for that matter. Much of it is referred to somewhere in the front part of this book but not explained, so here's explanation and amplification.

Suggested Individual One-Day Trip List

I have been paddling for years and I still sometimes wander off and forget something important when I fail to make a list of what I should take. While I realize everyone takes or wants different things, I believe most of the items below belong on almost any trip.

Summer

Rainsuit	8x8-foot plastic for rain tarp at lunch
Lunch	
Canteen	Matches (waterproof *and* in waterproof container)
Knee pads	
Life jacket	
Small trash bag with ties	Camera, smoking supplies, etc., as desired
Spare paddle	
Bailer and sponge	Waterproof container for day's equipment
Duct tape	
Throw rope	
First aid kit	String or cord for tying in

Winter

All of the Summer list, plus:

Complete change of clothes and small towel (unless it's a wet-suit day)
Space Blanket
Small stove (with fuel), cooking and eating utensils (or thermos with hot soup, etc.)

Shuttles

Shuttles are run before a trip starts so you have a vehicle waiting for you at the end of the trip. As obvious as this is, I have seen beginning canoeists completely baffled by the logistics involved. Shuttles, however, are really very simple. The primary idea is to have enough vehicles at the take-out to either load up all canoeists, their boats and gear, or to carry enough drivers back to the put-in to get their vehicles if most of the cars were left there.

The easiest and most common shuttle method is to meet at the put-in and have all unload their canoes and gear for the trip. Then, with only one person in each car (the drivers), the trip leader convoys all the cars down to the take-out where all are parked except just enough to cram all the drivers in and get them back to the put-in. It's best to leave the cars that have two-canoe racks at the take-out. Use the cars that can carry only one boat to take the drivers back to the put-in. At the end of the trip, load all the canoes and equipment into the waiting vehicles. If possible, some also load up the boats, gear, and drivers of the vehicles left up at the put-in and drive them back to their cars. Otherwise, somebody just takes these drivers back up, they drive back to the take-out, and load up. Someone stays with their equipment while all this is going on, of course.

This description supposes there is adequate parking at the take-out. If there's not and you must leave most of the vehicles at the put-in, still park as many cars as you can at the take-out but, at a minimum, enough to return one driver for each car you've left at the put-in *back* to the put-in at the end of the trip. This shuttle method isn't as efficient as it requires more driving and more time, but it's often necessary.

It's not necessary, of course, to meet at the put-in. The route to the river may be such that it's easier to meet at the take-out, drop off a few cars, combine boats and gear, and go on to the put-in. Circumstances, of course, will always dictate the actual shuttle machinery. Possibly the shuttle roads are really bad and some vehicles can't make it or any one of a dozen other reasons may require some shuttle modification.

Did I mention it's always nice for the trip leader, or whoever leads

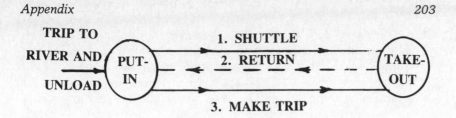

TRIP TO RIVER AND UNLOAD → PUT-IN

1. SHUTTLE →

2. RETURN ← ←

3. MAKE TRIP →

TAKE-OUT

A TYPICAL SHUTTLE

the shuttle, to know the way from the put-in to the take-out? It's embarrassing to get a long line of vehicles lost out on the back roads somewhere. I know – I've done it!

River and Paddler Classifications

An honest evaluation of your paddling skills can go a long way toward making you a better paddler *and* keeping you out of trouble on the river. Overrating your skills can lead to dangerous mismatches between you and the waters you attempt. The guides below will help you avoid some of these mismatches.

The first two charts are ratings for water and paddler classification. They are used courtesy of the American Whitewater Affiliation. As of this writing, copies of both charts and the safety code may be obtained from:

> The American Whitewater Affiliation
> 146 North Brockway
> Palatine, IL 60067

International Scale of River Difficulty

Class 1: *Easy.* Fast-moving water with riffles and small waves. Few obstructions, all obvious and easily missed with little training. Risk to swimmers is slight; self-rescue is easy.

Class 2: *Novice.* Straightforward rapids with wide, clear channels which are evident without scouting. Occasional maneuvering may be required, but rocks and medium-sized waves are easily missed by trained paddlers. Swimmers are seldom injured, and group assistance, while helpful, is seldom needed.

Class 3: Intermediate. Rapids with moderate, irregular waves which
may be difficult to avoid and which can swamp an open canoe.
Complex maneuvers in fast current and good boat control in tight
passages or around ledges are often required; large waves or
strainers may be present but are easily avoided. Strong eddies
and powerful current effects can be found, particularly on large-
volume rivers. Scouting is advisable for inexperienced parties.
Injuries while swimming are rare; self-rescue is usually easy but
group assistance may be required to avoid long swims.

Class 4: Advanced. Intense, powerful but predictable rapids requiring
precise boat handling in turbulent water. Depending on the char-
acter of the river, it may feature large, unavoidable waves and
holes or constricted passages demanding fast maneuvers under
pressure. A fast, reliable eddy turn may be needed to initiate
maneuvers, scout rapids, or rest. Rapids may require "must"
moves above dangerous hazards. Scouting is necessary the first
time down. Risk of injury to swimmers is moderate to high, and
water conditions may make self-rescue difficult. Group assistance
for rescue is often essential but requires practiced skills. A strong
eskimo roll is highly recommended.

Class 5: Expert. Extremely long, obstructed, or very violent rapids
which expose a paddler to above-average endangerment. Drops
may contain large, unavoidable waves and holes or steep, con-
gested chutes with complex, demanding routes. Rapids may continue for long distances between pools, demanding a high level of
fitness. What eddies exist may be small, turbulent, or difficult to
reach. At the high end of the scale, several of these factors may be
combined. Scouting is mandatory but often difficult. Swims are
dangerous, and rescue is difficult even for experts. A very reliable
eskimo roll, proper equipment, extensive experience, and practical rescue skills are essential for survival.

Class 6: Extreme. One grade more difficult than Class 5. These runs
often exemplify the extremes of difficulty, unpredictability and
danger. The consequences of errors are very severe and rescue
may be impossible. For teams of experts only, at favorable water
levels, after close personal inspection and taking all precautions.
This class does *not* represent drops thought to be unrunnable, but
may include rapids which are only occasionally run.

Of course these classifications are all a matter of water level, volume, and individual opinion, but maybe these accepted standards will

help you form your own educated estimate. In the western United States, the ratings of the rapids are usually graduated over a ten-level system instead of stopping at Class 6.

Guideline of Paddler Classification

Ratings for the comparative ability of paddlers were developed along with the water ratings.

Grade 1: *A Beginner.* Knows all basic strokes and can handle the boat competently in smooth water.

Grade 2: *A Novice.* Can use effectively all basic whitewater strokes in the kayak or in both bow and stern of the canoe. Can read water and negotiate rapids with assurance.

Grade 3: *An Intermediate.* Can negotiate rapids requiring complex sequential maneuvering. Can use eddy turn and basic bow-upstream techniques, is skillful in both bow and stern of double canoe, and single in canoe or kayak, in intermediate rapids.

Grade 4: *An Expert.* Has proven ability to run difficult rapids in both bow and stern of double canoe, and single in canoe or kayak. Has skill in heavy water and complex rapids.

Grade 5: *A Senior Leader.* In addition to expert canoeing skills, has wide experience and good judgment for leading trips on any river.

Another System

This system uses two ratings also but is much more precise, as you can tell by looking at it. The end result of each rating sheet is a number at which you arrive by *honestly* evaluating yourself and the river. By comparing your paddler number with the river number, you can arrive at a better conclusion about your ability to handle a particular rapid. If your rating is higher than the river's, it's a good indication that you can successfully handle the run with due attention to normal canoeing safety rules. If the river outrates you, it indicates a mismatch in favor of the river. In case of even numbers or close to it, use your best judgment, with consideration to the safety setup on the run and the abilities of the other trip participants. Some rivers or rapids, incidentally, have already been assigned their numbers. The Keel-Haulers Chart is used courtesy of the Keel Haulers Canoe Club of Northeast Ohio, and the author of the charts, John A. Kobak. The other chart is courtesy of the AWA.

KEEL-HAULER'S SELF-RATING SYSTEM

Total your score for each category to arrive at your own personal rating. Your score should also take into account the type of boat you are paddling. Then compare your rating to the approximate river rating chart. If your score is more than three points lower than the river you are considering, second thoughts should be given to the risks involved to yourself and other members of your group.

Activity	0 Points	1 Point	2 Points	3 Points
1. Swimming ability	Cannot swim	Weak swimmer	Average swimmer	Strong swimmer or skin diver
2. Stamina	Runs mile slower than 10 min.	Run mile in 8–10 minutes	Run mile in 6–8 minutes	Run faster than 5½-min. mile
3. Upper body strength	Cannot do 15 pushups	Can do 15 pushups/ 1–5 chinups	Can do 30 pushups/ 6–10 chinups	Can do 50 pushups/ 15 chinups
4. Equipment: Open boat or Decked boat	Canoe, 16′ tandem or 15′ solo	Canoe, 16′ tandem or 15′ solo, painters	Keelless whitewater canoe with extra flotation	
	No spray skirt or foot braces	Fully equipped fold boat or decked without full flotation	Fully outfitted with maximum flotation	Fiberglass or Kevlar only, with foam walls and split air bags
5. Experience in rated boat	Basic paddling skills	1 year of whitewater, 10 days paddling Class 2 or better	2–4 years of whitewater, paddle 10 days per year in Class 3	5 years whitewater, paddle 20 days per year in Class 3
6. Reading water	Can't read water well	Can pick route in Class 2 rapids	Can confidently lead in continuous Class 2 and scout best route in Class 3	Can confidently lead in continuous Class 3 and scout best route in Class 4 and 5
7. Boat control	Can control canoe from one side	Can maneuver in Class 2 avoiding big obstacles	Can maneuver in Class 3, know how to work with current	Finesse in boat placement in all types of water
8. Aggressiveness	Does not play	Timid, plays a little	Plays a lot in Class 3 water	Plays in Class 4 water with confidence
9. Eddy turns	Some difficulty in Class 2	Makes turns in and out of eddies from either side	Makes turns in and out of medium-size eddies in Class 3	Can catch small eddies in continuous Class 3–4

Activity	0 Points	1 Point	2 Points	3 Points
10. Ferrying	Cannot ferry	Can ferry upstream in Class 2	Can ferry upstream in Class 3 and downstream in Class 2	Can ferry upstream and downstream in Class 3 and 4
11. Hydraulic playing and bracing	Has difficulty in Class 2	Can play in small reversals and brace in Class 2 water	Can surf large hydraulics and effectively brace in Class 3 with small vertical drops	Can surf without paddle and brace in Class 4 with 4-foot vertical drops
12. Rescue ability	Self-rescue in flatwater	Can rescue self and others in Class 2	Can rescue self and others in Class 3	Can assist in rescues in Class 4 and 5
13. Rolling ability	Can't roll	Can roll in pool and 50% of time in Class 1	Can roll 3 out of 4 times in Class 3	Can roll 4 out of 5 times in Class 4

Safety Code

This safety code should be followed on all trips, no matter how tame, until its use becomes automatic. It was developed over a period of time by canoeing experts from their own experiences and that of thousands of other canoeists.

River Signals

It's virtually impossible to yell loudly enough for anyone to hear you on a running river if they're very far away. It's equally impossible for you to hear what they're trying to tell you. Hand or paddle signals are the answer. Here are those adopted by the American Whitewater Affiliation and used here with their permission.

Throwing Rescue Ropes and Bags

Practice is the key to successful throwing of rescue ropes and bags. Both are simple to handle. At first glance, the rescue bag will appear to be much the easier. I recommend you learn to handle both ropes and bags. I also recommend you try your hand at catching someone on a line and experience being caught by one before you really need to do either.

DIFFICULTY RATING CHART FOR RIVER SECTIONS OR INDIVIDUAL RAPIDS

Prepared by Guidebook Committee, American White-Water Affiliation – H. J. Wilhoyte February 12, 1956

	Factors Related Primarily to Success In Negotiation			Factors Affecting Both Success & Safety				Factors Related Primarily to Safe Rescue			
	SECONDARY FACTORS			PRIMARY FACTORS				SECONDARY FACTORS			
POINTS	Bends	Length, Ft.	Gradient, Ft./Mi.	Obstacles Rocks, Trees	Waves	Turbulence	Resting or Rescue Spots	Water Velocity	Width, Depth	Water Temperature	Accessibility
NONE	Few Very gradual	Less than 100	Less than 5 regular slope	None	Few inches high Avoidable	None	Almost any-where	Less than 3 mph.	Narrow <75' & Shallow <3'	>65°F	Road along river
1	Many Gradual	100–700	5–15 Regular	Few: Passage almost straight through	Low (Up to 1') Regular avoid-able	Minor ed-dies		3–6 mph	Wide >75' & Shallow <3'	55°–65°F	One hour travel by foot or water
2	Few Sharp-Blind Scouting nec-essary	700–5000	15–40 Ledges or steep drops	Courses easily recog-nizable	Low to medium (Up to 3') Regular Avoidable	Medium ed-dies		6–10 mph	Narrow <75' & Deep >3'	45°–55°F	One hour to one day travel by foot or water
3		5000+	40+ Steep drops Small falls	Maneuvering required. Course not easily recog-nizable	Medium to large (Up to 5') Mostly recog-nizable Avoidable	Strong ed-dies Cross cur-rents	A good one below every danger spot	>10 mph or flood	Wide >75' & Deep >3'	<45°F	One day travel by foot or water
4				Intricate maneuvering Course hard to recognize	Large-Irregular Avoidable or me-dium to large Unavoidable	Very strong eddies Strong cross currents					
5				Course tor-turous Frequent scouting	Large Irregular Unavoidable	Large-scale eddies and cross cur-rents, some up and down cur-rents				Ice forms on boat	
6				Very tor-turous Always scout from shore	Very large (>5') Irregular Unavoidable Special equip-ment required	Very large scale Strong up and down currents	Almost none				

Universal River Signals (Used by courtesy of the AWA)

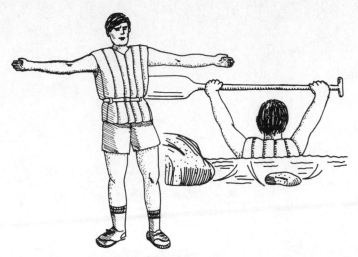

STOP: Potential hazard ahead. Wait for "all clear" signal before proceeding, or scout ahead. Those seeing the signal should pass it back to others in the party.

HELP/EMERGENCY: Assist the signaller as quickly as possible. Give three long blasts on a police whistle while waving a paddle, life vest, or helmet over your head. If a whistle is not available, use the visual signal alone.

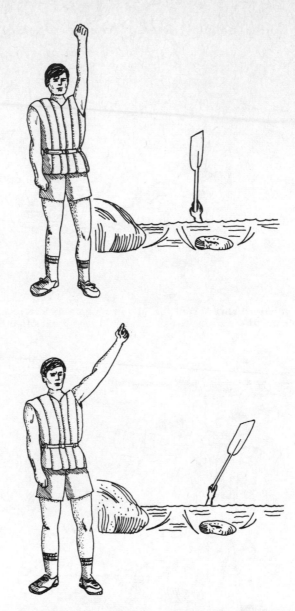

ALL CLEAR: Come ahead (in the absence of other directions), proceed down the center. Form a vertical bar with your paddle or one arm held high above your head. Paddle blade should be turned flat for maximum visibility. To signal direction or a preferred course through a rapid around obstructions, lower the previously vertical "all clear" by 45 degrees toward the side of the river with the preferred route. Never point toward the obstacle you wish to avoid.

Here are the fundamentals:

Don't throw the entire rope to the swimmer! As silly as this may sound, I've seen it done many times. Keep a firm grip on your end of the rope.

Don't get pulled into the river yourself. Find as secure a spot as you can to stand; in shallow water near the shore or out on a rock is preferable to a muddy shoreline. If you can't find a good place to stand, have a "human chain" ready, someone behind you to hold your waist, someone behind that person, etc.

Don't get your rope tangled in trees or bushes when you throw it. Find as clear a spot as possible and be aware of nearby bushes and overhanging tree limbs.

Do "lead" the swimmer by aiming the rope downstream. The rope takes a second or two to uncoil and the current is moving the swimmer. Aim far enough ahead so rope and swimmer arrive at the same place at the same time. The farther he is from the shore and the faster he's moving, the more lead you give. This is a matter of practice and experience.

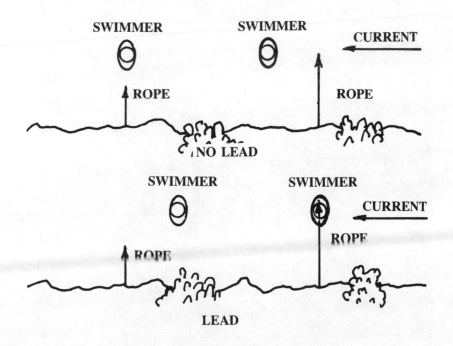

"LEADING" WITH A RESCUE LINE

Throwing the Rescue Bag (For Right-handed Throwers)

Untie the bag (not necessary if the bag top is open enough for the rope in it to come out freely). Pull out a few feet of rope and hold the free end in your left hand. Grasp the bag top with your right hand.

Throw the bag with a smooth underhand, sidearm, or overhand motion, whichever you find easiest. The rope will pull out of the bag as it flies through the air.

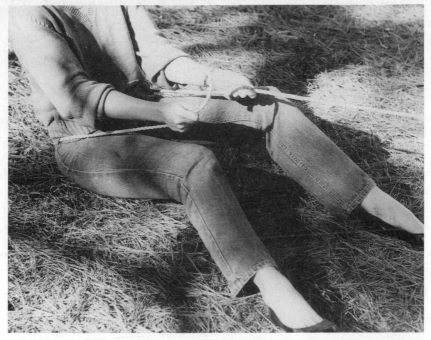

Belay.

Do throw over (beyond) the swimmer so the rope goes up in an arc then falls to the water. Throwing straight at the swimmer probably means you'll miss.

Do "belay" as soon as you throw. The swimmer's weight and speed on the end of a suddenly taut rope can easily pull you in the river too. Before the slack comes out, lay the rope around your waist and sit down with the rope running out between your outstretched and braced legs *in the direction of the pull*. If the pull is to your side, it could roll you over. If you have the rope up on your shoulders or upper back, it could injure as well as unbalance you. Move the rope to belay position *behind* you at waist level. Never lift it up over your head and bring it down behind you. You may have too little time and the pull come when the rope is behind your neck.

To rethrow, pull the rope back in, letting it fall to the ground at your feet. Try not to tangle it and don't step on it. *Don't* stuff it back in the bag. If you need to rethrow, the water caught in the bag will make this throw easier. You may need to pour out some of the water if the bag is too full of it.

Throwing the Rescue Rope (For Right-handed Throwers)

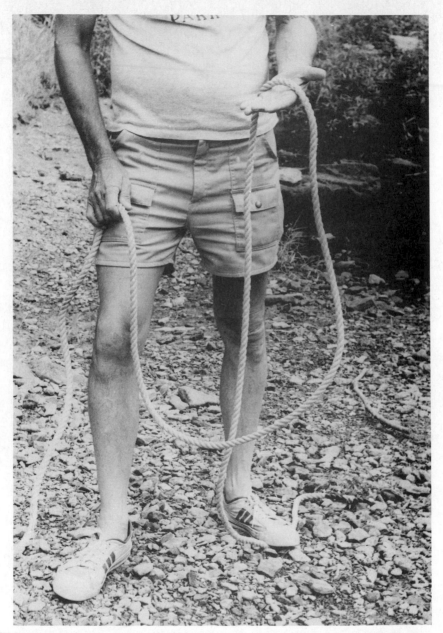

Untie the rope, drop one end, and stand on it with your left foot, letting the rope run over the palm of your left hand and under your left thumb.

Coil the rope in a clockwise direction, laying the coils neatly side by side in your left hand, as much as your hand size will allow. Make the coils as big as you can handle without their dragging. If necessary, make a small coil of the final few feet of rope—don't let it hang loose. (With twisted construction rope, give the rope a half twist in a clockwise direction as you coil it. This removes its tendency to form figure 8 coils instead of round ones.)

Separate the coils into two halves with only a single rope connecting the halves. Two or more connecting ropes means a tangle.

With the left hand coils in your open left hand and your left thumb over the rope going to your foot, sling the right hand coils with a sideways motion. As these coils fly out, they will uncoil the rope in your left hand.

To store the rope, just put it back in the bag; it's not necessary to coil it. Leave the mouth of the bag open about one inch after the rope is in it.

The belay is the same as for the rescue rope. To rethrow: pull the rope back in, coiling it as you do, and give the rope a half twist with each coil if necessary.

Canoe-Over-Canoe Rescue

Generally a solo boat can simply be pulled into a shallow part of the river or up on a rock or the bank and emptied of water. With a lot of flotation it can also be bailed empty in a few minutes. For those wider river stretches, however, here's a time-honored technique that's effective (if a little tricky) in a full-fledged slalom canoe. Remember this is an unobstructed part of the river technique; it's *not* to be tried in the middle of a rapid!

Canoe-Over-Canoe Rescue

Position the rescue canoe upstream of the swamped canoe. If possible, the dumped canoeist should get on the upstream side of the rescue boat and help balance it.

Roll the swamped canoe over, bottom-up, break any vacuum under the hull by raising one gunwale slightly out of the water, and pull the upside-down canoe across the rescue canoe. It will empty as you do this.

Flip the rescued canoe right-side-up and slide it back in the water downstream and alongside the rescue canoe.

Balance the rescued canoe while the paddler gets back in it.

Glossary

These terms are sprinkled through the book. Although very little in this world is absolutely definite, the meanings I have assigned are generally accepted by most paddlers. You'll be speaking the language, if not the exact dialect.

AFT   A direction. That part of the canoe behind the paddler.

BEAM   The widest point of a canoe hull.

BILGE   The rounded part of a canoe hull between the bottom and the side.

BLADE   See Paddle.

BOW   The front end of a canoe.

BROACH   To turn sideways in the trough of a wave.

COCKPIT   The open hole in a spray skirt where the paddler sits, also the open center of a solo canoe between the flotation.

DEPTH   The distance between the lowest point of the gunwale and the lowest point of the bottom of the hull.

FACE   See Paddle.

FEATHER (FEATHERED)   The position of a paddle blade in many stroke recoveries. The blade is parallel to the water so wind and wave impact (or water, in an underwater recovery) strikes the edge rather than the flat of the blade.

FLOTATION   Buoyant material installed in a canoe hull to keep water out.

FORE (FORWARD)   A direction. That part of the canoe in front of the paddler.

GRIP   See Paddle.

GUNWALE   The part of the canoe encircling the open top of the hull.

HEEL   The rolling of a canoe hull to either side along its longitudinal centerline. Also called roll.

HULL   The basic body of the canoe.

INBOARD   Anything located or positioned between the gunwales, as opposed to out over the water.

KEEL   The real piece or imaginary line down the bottom, longitudinal centerline of the canoe hull.

LATERAL   A direction to the side of the canoe.

LONGITUDINAL   A direction along the length of the canoe.

LOWER HAND   The hand gripping the paddle nearest the blade.

NON-POWER FACE   See Power face.

OFF SIDE   A technique done *opposite to* the side on which you are paddling but *without* changing hand positions on the paddle.

ON SIDE   A technique done on the same side as you are paddling.

PADDLE   The tool used to propel the canoe. A paddle consists of a grip, shaft, throat, and blade. The flat part of the blade is called the face, the thin edge the edge, and the end the tip. See the illustrations in Chapter 3.

PAINTER   A rope attached to the bow and stern of a canoe for tying it down during transport.

PFD   A personal flotation device, a life jacket.

PITCH   The tilting forward and backward of a canoe hull along its lateral centerline.

POWER FACE (NON-POWER FACE)   The power face of a paddle is that face of the blade pushing against the water in a normal forward stroke. The Non-power face is the other side of the blade during this stroke.

PUT-IN   The location of the start of a canoe trip.

RECOVERY   The return of the paddle from the end of one stroke to the beginning of another stroke, whether this be underwater or above the water.

ROCKER   The upward curvature of the keel of a canoe toward the bow and stern, generally beginning at the lateral centerline.

ROLL   See Heel.

SHAFT   See Paddle.

SLALOM   A canoe designed for quick maneuvering. Also the name of a canoe competition in which the canoes must make quick maneuvers through obstacles.

SOLO   One paddler in a canoe.

STERN   The back end of a canoe.

STRAINER   An obstruction in a river through which water can flow, but which is too small for a canoe or body to pass through. A common example is a downed tree with branches in the water.

SWAMPING   The filling of the entire hull with water.

TAKE-OUT   The location of the end of a canoe trip.

TANDEM   Two paddlers in a canoe.

THROAT   See Paddle.

THWART   A canoe part running laterally from gunwale to gunwale.

TIP   See Paddle.

TRACK   The tendency of a canoe to remain in its path when propelled by a paddle stroke. Slalom and factory solo boats have little tracking ability.

TUMBLEHOME   The inward curve on the upper sides of some canoes caused by the difference in width between the beam and the canoe's width at the widest point of the gunwales.

UPPER HAND   The hand holding the grip of the paddle.

YAW   The side-to-side motion of the canoe around its *vertical* centerline.

AMERICAN WHITEWATER AFFILIATION
SAFETY CODE

I. Personal Preparedness and Responsibility
   1. *Be a competent swimmer,* with the ability to handle yourself underwater.
   2. *Wear a life jacket.* A snugly fitting vest-type life preserver offers back and shoulder protection as well as the flotation needed to swim safely in whitewater.
   3. *Wear a solid, correctly fitted helmet* when upsets are likely. This is essential in kayaks or covered canoes, and recommended for open canoeists using thigh straps and rafters running steep drops.
   4. *Do not boat out of control.* Your skills should be sufficient to stop or reach shore before reaching danger. Do not enter a rapid unless you are reasonably sure that you can run it safely or swim it without injury.
   5. *Whitewater rivers contain many hazards that are not always easily recognized. The following are the most frequent killers:*
      a. *High water.* The river's speed and power increase tremendously as the flow increases, raising the difficulty of most rapids. Rescue becomes progressively harder as the water rises, adding to the danger. Floating debris and strainers make even an easy rapid quite hazardous. It is often misleading to judge the river level at the put-in, since a small rise in a wide, shallow place will be multiplied many times where the river narrows. Use reliable gauge information whenever possible, and be aware that sun on snowpack, hard rain, and upstream dam releases may greatly increase the flow.
      b. *Cold.* Cold drains your strength, and robs you of the ability to make sound decisions on matters affecting your survival. Cold-water immersion, because of the initial shock and the rapid heat loss that follows, is especially dangerous. Dress appropriately for bad weather or sudden immersion in the water. When the water temperature is less than 50 degrees F, a wetsuit or drysuit is essential for protection if you swim. Next best is wool or pile clothing under a waterproof shell. In this case, you should also carry waterproof matches and a change of clothing in a waterproof bag. If, after prolonged expo-

sure, a person experiences uncontrollable shaking, loss of coordination, or difficulty speaking, he or she is hypothermic and needs your assistance.

c. *Strainers.* Brush, fallen trees, bridge pilings, undercut rocks, or anything else which allows river current to sweep through can pin boats and boaters against the obstacle. Water pressure on anything trapped this way can be overwhelming. Rescue is often extremely difficult. Pinning may occur in fast current, with little or no whitewater to warn of the danger.

d. *Dams, weirs, ledges, reversals, holes, and hydraulics.* When water drops over an obstacle, it curls back on itself, forming a strong upstream current which may be capable of holding a boat or a swimmer. Some holes make for excellent sport; others are proven killers. Paddlers who cannot recognize the differences should avoid all but the smallest holes. Hydraulics around man-made dams must be treated with utmost respect regardless of their height or the level of the river. Despite their seemingly benign appearance, they can create an almost escape-proof trap. The swimmer's only exit from the "drowning machine" is to dive below the surface when the downstream current is flowing beneath the reversal.

e. *Broaching.* When a boat is pushed sideways against a rock by strong current, it may collapse and wrap. This is especially dangerous to kayak and decked-canoe paddlers; these boats will collapse and the combination of indestructible hulls and tight outfitting may create a deadly trap. Even without entrapment, releasing pinned boats can be extremely time-consuming and dangerous. To avoid pinning, throw your weight downstream toward the rock. This allows the current to slide harmlessly underneath the hull.

6. *Boating alone* is discouraged. The minimum party is three people or two craft.

7. *Have a frank knowledge of your boating ability,* and don't attempt rivers or rapids which lie beyond that ability.

a. Develop the paddling skills and teamwork required to match the river you plan to boat. Most good paddlers develop skills gradually, and attempts to advance too quickly will compromise your safety and enjoyment.

    b. Be in good physical and mental condition, consistent with the difficulties which may be expected. Make adjustments for loss of skills due to age, health, fitness. Any health limitations must be explained to your fellow paddlers prior to starting the trip.

8. *Be practiced in self-rescue,* including escape from an overturned craft. The Eskimo Roll is strongly recommended for decked boaters who run rapids of Class 4 or greater, or who paddle in cold environmental conditions.

9. *Be trained in rescue skills,* CPR, and first aid, with special emphasis on recognizing and treating hypothermia. It may save your friend's life.

10. *Carry equipment needed for unexpected emergencies,* including footwear which will protect your feet when walking out, a throw rope, knife, whistle and waterproof matches. If you wear eyeglasses, tie them on and carry a spare pair on long trips. Bring cloth repair tape on short runs, and a full repair kit on isolated rivers. Do not wear bulky jackets, ponchos, heavy boots, or anything else which could reduce your ability to survive a swim.

11. *Despite the mutually supportive group structure described in this code, individual paddlers are ultimately responsible for their own safety, and must assume sole responsibility for the following decisions:*

    a. The decision to participate on any trip. This includes an evaluation of the expected difficulty of the rapids under the conditions existing at the time of the put-in.

    b. The selection of appropriate equipment, including a boat design suited to their skills and the appropriate rescue and survival gear.

    c. The decision to scout any rapid, and to run or portage according to their best judgement. Other members of the group may offer advice, but paddlers should resist pressure from anyone to paddle beyond their skills. It is also their responsibility to decide whether to pass up any walk-out or take-out opportunity.

    d. All trip participants should constantly evaluate their own and their group's safety, voicing their concerns when appropriate and following what they believe to be the best course of action. Paddlers are encouraged to speak with anyone whose actions on the water are dangerous, whether they are a part of your group or not.

II. *Boat and Equipment Preparedness*

1. *Test new and different equipment* under familiar conditions before relying on it for difficult runs. This is especially true when adopting a new boat design or outfitting system. Low-volume craft may present additional hazards to inexperienced or poorly conditioned paddlers.

2. *Be sure your boat and gear* are in good repair before starting a trip. The more isolated and difficult the run, the more rigorous this inspection should be.

3. *Install flotation bags* in non-inflatable craft, securely fixed in each end, designed to displace as much water as possible. Inflatable boats should have multiple air chambers and be test inflated before launching.

4. *Have strong, properly sized paddles or oars* for controlling your craft. Carry sufficient spares for the length and difficulty of the trip.

5. *Outfit your boat safely.* The ability to exit your boat quickly is an essential component of safety in rapids. It is your responsibility to see that there is absolutely nothing to cause entrapment when coming free of an upset craft. This includes:

   a. Spray covers which won't release reliably or which release prematurely.

   b. Boat outfitting too tight to allow a fast exit, especially in low-volume kayaks or decked canoes. This includes low-hung thwarts in canoes lacking adequate clearance for your feet and kayak footbraces which fail or allow your feet to become wedged under them.

   c. Inadequately supported decks which collapse on a paddler's legs when a decked boat is pinned by water pressure. Inadequate clearance with the deck because of your size or build.

   d. Loose ropes which cause entanglement. Beware of any length of loose line attached to a whitewater boat. All items must be tied tightly and excess line eliminated; painters, throw lines, and safety rope systems must be completely and effectively stored. Do not knot the end of a rope, as it can get caught in cracks between rocks.

6. *Provide ropes* which permit you to hold on to your craft so that it may be rescued. The following methods are recommended:

   a. Kayaks and covered canoes should have grab loops of ¼″ + rope or equivalent webbing sized to admit a normal-sized hand. Stern painters are permissible if properly secured.

   b. Open canoes should have securely anchored bow and stern painters consisting of 8–10 feet of ¼" + line. These must be secured in such a way that they are readily accessible, but cannot come loose accidentally. Grab loops are acceptable, but are more difficult to reach after an upset.

   c. Rafts and dories may have taut perimeter lines threaded through the loops provided. Footholds should be designed so that a paddler's feet cannot be forced through them, causing entrapment. Flip lines should be carefully and reliably stowed.

  7. *Know your craft's carrying capacity,* and how added loads affect boat handling in whitewater. Most rafts have a minimum crew size, which can be added to on day trips or in easy rapids. Carrying more than two paddlers in an open canoe when running rapids is not recommended.

  8. *Car-top racks* must be strong and attach positively to the vehicle. Lash your boat to each crossbar, then tie the ends of the boats directly to the bumpers for added security. This arrangement should survive all but the most violent vehicle accident.

III. Group Preparedness and Responsibility

  1. *Organization.* River trips should be regarded as common adventures by all participants, except on specially designated instructional or guided trips. The group is collectively responsible for the conduct of the trip, and participants are individually responsible for judging their own capabilities and for their own safety as the trip progresses.

  2. *River Conditions.* The group should have a reasonable knowledge of the difficulty of the run. Participants should evaluate this information and adjust their plans accordingly. If the run is exploratory or no one is familiar with the river, maps and guidebooks, if available, should be examined. The group should secure accurate flow information; the more difficult the run, the more important this will be. Be aware of possible changes in river level and how this will affect the difficulty of the run. If the trip involves tidal stretches, secure appropriate information on tides.

  3. *Group equipment should be suited to the difficulty of the river.* The group should always have a throw line available, and

one line per boat is recommended on difficult runs. The list may include: carabiners, prussick loops, first aid kit, flashlight, folding saw, fire starter, guidebooks, maps, food, extra clothing, and any other rescue or survival items suggested by conditions. Each item is not required on every run, and this list is not meant to be a substitute for good judgement.

4. *Keep the group compact,* but maintain sufficient spacing to avoid collisions. If the group is large, consider dividing into smaller groups or using the "Buddy System" as an additional safeguard. Space yourselves closely enough to permit good communication, but not so close as to interfere with one another in rapids.

   a. *The lead paddler* sets the pace. When in front, do not get in over your head. Never run drops when you cannot see a clear route to the bottom or, for advanced paddlers, a sure route to the next eddy. When in doubt, stop and scout.

   b. *Keep track* of all group members. Each boat keeps the one behind it in sight, stopping if necessary. Know how many people are in your group and take head counts regularly. No one should paddle ahead or walk out without first informing the group. Weak paddlers should stay at the center of a group, and not allow themselves to lag behind. If the group is large and contains a wide range of abilities, a designated "Sweep Boat" should bring up the rear.

   c. *Courtesy.* On heavily used rivers, do not cut in front of a boater running a drop. Always look upstream before leaving eddies to run or play. Never enter a crowded drop or eddy when no room for you exists. Passing other groups in a rapid may be hazardous; it's often safer to wait upstream until the group ahead has passed.

5. *Float plan.* If the trip is into a wilderness area or for an extended period, plans should be filed with a responsible person who will contact the authorities if you are overdue. It may be wise to establish checkpoints along the way where civilization could be contacted if necessary. Knowing the location of possible help and preplanning escape routes can speed rescue.

6. *Drugs.* The use of alcohol or mind-altering drugs before or during river trips is not recommended. It dulls reflexes, re-

duces decision-making ability, and may interfere with important survival reflexes.

7. *Instruction or guided trips.* In this format, a person assumes the responsibilities of a trip leader. He or she may pass judgment on a participant's qualifications, check equipment, and assume responsibilities for the conduct of the trip normally taken by the group as a whole.

   a. These trips must be clearly designated as such in advance, as they could expose the leader to legal liability. Trip or personal liability insurance should be considered.

   b. Even on trips with a designated leader, participants must recognize that whitewater rivers have inherent hazards, that each person is still responsible for the decision to participate and their safety on the water.

IV. Guidelines for River Rescue

1. *Recover from an upset with an Eskimo Roll* whenever possible. Evacuate your boat immediately if there is imminent danger of being trapped against rocks, brush, or any other kind of strainer.

2. *If you swim, hold on to your boat.* It has much flotation and is easy for rescuers to spot. Get to the upstream end so that you cannot be crushed between a rock and your boat by the force of the current. Persons with good balance may be able to climb on top of a swamped kayak or flipped raft and paddle to shore.

3. *Release your craft if this will improve your chances,* especially if the water is cold or dangerous rapids lie ahead. Actively attempt self-rescue whenever possible by swimming for safety. Be prepared to assist others who may come to your aid.

   a. *When swimming in shallow or obstructed* rapids, lie on your back *with feet held high* and pointed downstream. Do not attempt to stand in fast-moving water; if your foot wedges on the bottom, fast water will push you under and keep you there. Get to slow or very shallow water before attempting to stand or walk. Look ahead! Avoid possible pinning situations including undercut rocks, strainers, downed trees, holes, and other dangers by swimming away from them.

   b. *If the rapids are deep and powerful,* roll over onto your stomach and swim aggressively for shore. Watch for eddies and slackwater and use them to get out of the current. Strong swimmers can effect a powerful upstream ferry and get to shore fast. If the shores are obstructed with strainers or undercut rocks, however, it is safer to "ride the rapid out" until a safer escape can be found.

4. *If others spill and swim,* go after the boaters first. Rescue boats and equipment only if this can be done safely. While participants usually assist one another to the best of their ability, they should do so only if they can, in their judgement, do so safely. The first duty of a rescuer is not to compound the problem by becoming another victim.

5. *The use of rescue lines requires training;* uninformed use may cause injury. Never tie yourself into either end of a line without a reliable quick-release system. Have a knife handy to deal with unexpected entanglement. Learn to place set lines effectively, to throw accurately, to belay effectively, and to properly handle a rope thrown to you.

6. *When reviving a drowning victim,* be aware that cold water may greatly extend survival time underwater. Victims of hypothermia may have depressed vital signs so they look and feel dead. Don't give up; continue CPR for as long as possible without compromising safety.

Index